EARTHEN VESSELS

GABRIEL BUNGE, O.S.B.

Earthen Vessels

The Practice of Personal Prayer
According to the Patristic Tradition

Translated by
Michael J. Miller

Pen and ink drawings by
Francesco Riganti

IGNATIUS PRESS   SAN FRANCISCO

Original German edition:
*Irdene Gefäße: Die Praxis des persönlichen Gebetes
nach der Überlieferung der heiligen Väter*
© 1996 Verlag "Der Christliche Osten" GmbH, Würzburg

Cover art by Francesco Riganti

Cover design by Roxanne Mei Lum

© 2002 Ignatius Press, San Francisco
All rights reserved
ISBN 978–0–89870–837–0
Library of Congress Control Number 00–109337
Printed in the United States of America ∞

CONTENTS

Do not merely speak with pleasure
about the deeds of the Fathers,
but demand of yourself also the
accomplishment of the same amid great labors.

— Evagrius Ponticus

INTRODUCTION

"Lord, teach us to pray"

(Lk 11:1)

In ecclesiastical circles today one often hears the lament, "The faith is evaporating." Despite an unprecedented "pastoral approach", the faith of many Christians in fact appears to be "growing cold"[1] or even, to put it colloquially, to be "evaporating". There is talk of a great crisis of faith, among the clergy no less than among the laity.

This loss of faith, which is so often lamented in the West, stands nevertheless in contrast to a seemingly paradoxical fact: This same Western world is simultaneously producing an immense stream of theological and, above all, spiritual literature, which swells year after year with thousands of new titles. To be sure, among them are many ephemeral fads created solely to be marketed. Yet numerous classical works of spirituality, too, are being critically edited and translated into all the European languages, so that the modern reader has available to him a wealth of spiritual writings that no one in antiquity would even have dreamed of.

This abundance would really have to be taken as the sign of an unprecedented flourishing of the spiritual life—were it not for the aforementioned loss of faith. This flood of books, therefore, is probably rather the sign of a restless search that

[1] Cf. Mt 24:12.

still somehow does not seem to reach its goal. Many, of course, read these writings, and they may also marvel at the wisdom of the Fathers—yet in their personal lives nothing changes. Somehow the key to these treasures of tradition has been lost. Scholars speak in this regard of a *break in tradition*, which has opened up a chasm between the present and the past.

Many sense this, even if they are unable to formulate the problem as such. A feeling of discontent grips ever-larger circles. People look for a way out of the spiritual crisis, which many then think they have found (appealing to a very broad notion of ecumenism) in an openness to the non-Christian religions. The extremely wide assortment of "spiritual masters" of various schools makes easier that first step beyond the boundaries of one's own religion, in a way that the readers do not suspect. Then, too, those who are searching hungrily encounter a gigantic market of literature, ranging from the "spiritual" through the "esoteric". And many think that they have even found there what they had looked for in vain within Christianity, or else what was supposedly never there in the first place.

It is by no means our intention to do battle with this sort of "ecumenism". We will only formulate a few questions at the end and briefly sketch the answer that the Fathers might well have given. This book is concerned with giving a genuinely *Christian answer* to the spiritual search of many believers. And a "practical" one, at that: that is, it should point out a "way"—rooted in Scripture and the original tradition—that enables a Christian to "practice" his *faith* in a *manner* that is in keeping with the *contents* of the faith.

For there is a very simple answer to the perplexing question, why the faith of an increasing number of Christians is "evaporating" despite all efforts to enliven it—an answer that perhaps does not contain the entire truth about the causes of the crisis, but which nonetheless indicates a way out. The faith "evaporates" when it is no longer *practiced*—in a way that accords with its essence. "Praxis" here does not mean the various forms of "social action" that perennially have been the obvious expression of Christian *agape*. However indispensable this "outreach" is, it becomes merely external, or (as a flight into activism) even a subtle form of *acedia*, of boredom,[2] whenever there is no longer any corresponding "reach within".

Prayer is the "interior striving" par excellence—prayer in the fullest sense acquired by this term in Scripture and tradition. "Tell me *how* you pray, and I will tell you *what* you believe", one could say, as a variation on a familiar adage. In prayer, right down to the practical methods of prayer, it becomes evident what constitutes the essence of being a Christian: how the believer stands in relation to God and to his neighbor.

Hence one can say, with some exaggeration: *Only in prayer is the Christian really himself.*

Christ himself is the best proof of this. For does not his essence, his unique relationship to God, whom he calls "my Father", become evident precisely in his prayer, as it is portrayed in the Synoptic Gospels with restraint and then by John with complete clarity? The disciples, in any case, understood this, and when they asked him, "Lord, teach us to pray", Jesus taught them the Our Father. Even before there was a Creed to sum up the Christian faith, this simple text epitomized what it means to be a Christian, precisely *in the form of a prayer*—that is to say, that new relationship

---

[2] Cf. Gabriel Bunge, *Akedia: Die geistliche Lehre des Evagrios Pontikos vom Überdruss*, 4th ed. (Würzburg, 1995).

between God and man which the only begotten, incarnate Son of God established in his own Person. This is certainly no coincidence.

~

The Bible teaches that man was *created* "in the image of God",[3] that is, as the Fathers profoundly interpret it, "as the image of the Divine Image" (Origen), of the Son, therefore, who alone is the "Image of God" in the absolute sense.[4] Man is *destined*, however, to be the "image and likeness" of God.[5] He is therefore designed with a view to *becoming*: specifically, he is meant to pass from being "in the image of God" over to the (eschatological) state of being "made like unto" the Son.[6]

From this creation "in the image of God" it follows that the most essential thing about man is that he is intrinsically *in relation* to God (Augustine), after the analogy of the relation between an original image and its copy. Yet this relation is not static, like the one between a seal and its impression, for instance, but rather living, dynamic, and fully realized only through becoming.

For man, this means concretely that he, by analogy to his Creator, possesses a *face*. Just as God—who is Person in the absolute sense and who alone is capable of creating personal being—possesses a "face", namely, his only begotten Son (which is why the Fathers simply equate the biblical expressions "the image of God" and "the face of God"), so too man, as a created personal being, has a "face".

[3] Gen 1:27.
[4] 2 Cor 4:4.
[5] Gen 1:26.
[6] 1 Jn 3:2.

The "face" is that "side" of the person that he turns toward another person when he enters into a personal relationship with the other. "Face" really means: *being turned toward*. Only a person can have, strictly speaking, a real "counterpart" to which he turns or from which he turns away. Being a person—and for man this always means becoming more and more a person—always comes about "face to face" with a counterpart. Therefore Paul contrasts our present, indirect knowledge of God, "in a mirror dimly [Greek: *en ainígmati* = enigmatically]", with the perfect eschatological beatitude in knowing God "face to face", whereby man "shall know as he is known".[7]

What is said here about the spiritual essence of man finds expression also in his corporeal nature. It is the bodily countenance in which this spiritual essence is reflected. To turn one's face toward another or deliberately to turn it away from him is not something indifferent, as everyone knows from daily experience, but rather a gesture of profound, symbolic meaning. Indeed, it indicates whether we want to enter into a personal relationship with another or want to deny him this.

The purest expression of this "being turned toward God" to be found here on earth is prayer, in which the creature does in fact "turn" toward his Creator, in those moments when the person at prayer "seeks the face of God"[8] and asks that the Lord might "let his face shine" upon him.[9] In these and similar phrases from the Book of Psalms, which are by no means merely poetic metaphors, the fundamental experience of biblical man is expressed, for whom God is

---

[7] 1 Cor 13:12.
[8] Ps 26:8 (LXX) = Ps 27:8 (RSV).
[9] Ps 79:4 (LXX) = Ps 80:3 (RSV).

not an abstract, impersonal principle, after all, but rather is Person in the absolute sense. God turns toward man, calls him to himself, and wants man to turn to him also. And man does this quintessentially in prayer, in which he, with both soul *and* body, "places himself in God's presence".

~

With that we have returned to the actual theme of this book: the practice or "praxis" of prayer. For "to learn to pray from the Lord", to pray as the men of the Bible and our Fathers in faith did, means not only making certain texts one's own, but also to assimilate all of those methods, forms, gestures, and so on, in which this praying finds *its most suitable expression.* This was, in any case, the opinion of the Fathers themselves, for whom this was by no means a matter of historically conditioned externals. On the contrary, they gave their full attention to these things, which Origen summarizes as follows at the end of his treatise *On Prayer.*

> *It seems to me [in light of the preceding] to be not inappropriate, in order to present exhaustively the subject of prayer, by way of an introduction, to examine [also] the [interior] disposition and the [exterior] posture that the person praying must have, as well as the place where one should pray, and the direction in which one must face in all circumstances, and the favorable time that is to be reserved for prayer, and whatever other similar things there may be.*[10]

Then Origen immediately *cites the Bible* to demonstrate that these questions are in fact not at all inappropriate, but are posed for us by Scripture itself. We, too, want to be guided by these signposts. In this regard we deliberately

---

[10] Origen, *De Oratione* 31, 1.

limit our subject to personal prayer, since that is the sure foundation not only of the spiritual life but also of liturgical prayer in common.

As the Fathers themselves knew better than anyone else, one must never take Scripture out of context if one wants to understand it correctly. For the Christian this context is the *Church*, and the apostolic and patristic tradition gives testimony to her life and her faith. As a consequence of those breaks in tradition which have accompanied the history of the Western Church in particular, this treasure has become practically inaccessible to many today. And this is so even though we have available today an unprecedented abundance of valuable editions and translations of patristic texts. The purpose of this book is, therefore, to put into the hands of the Christian of our time the key to these treasures.

The same key, this "praxis", by the way, opens the doors to other treasures as well, for instance of the liturgy, of art, and finally of theology also, in the original sense of this word as "speaking about God"—not on the basis of scientific study, but as the fruit of the most intimate familiarity.

> *The Lord's breast: the knowledge of God.*
> *Whoever rests on it will be a theologian.*[11]

~

Note: The Fathers generally used the ancient Greek translation of the Old Testament (Septuagint, abbreviated "LXX"), which therefore we in turn take as our basis, also with respect to the numbering of the psalms.

---

[11] Evagrius, *Ad Monachos* 120 (Gressmann).

Chapter I

"No one after drinking old wine desires new. . ."

(Lk 5:39)

Although, as we have explained, it is not our intention to write a historical or a patristic study on the subject of "prayer", in the following pages we will still refer again and again to the holy Fathers of the Church's early period. Resorting constantly to "that which was from the beginning" requires some justification in an age when people like to regard the novelty of a thing as a standard of its value. Here, however, it is not our purpose at all to bring the latest to the reader at the beginning of the twenty-first century, but instead to present, with respect to prayer, that which was "delivered to us by those who from the beginning were eyewitnesses and ministers of the word".[1] Why this high esteem for "what was handed down" and this unique rank that is accorded to the "beginning"? Or in a more personal vein, addressing the writer of these lines: Why does he not speak, rather, of his own experience, instead of bringing up his holy Fathers all the time?

It might therefore be useful to explain right away in what "spirit" this book was written, how it is to be read, as well as to shed some light on the broader context in which prayer,

[1] Cf. Lk 1:2.

too, belongs and which provides the only possible framework for understanding it correctly.

~

1. *"That which was from the beginning"* (1 Jn 1:1)

Constant recourse to the sayings of the holy Fathers has its basis in the nature and meaning of what the oldest witnesses from apostolic times, in Sacred Scripture itself, call "tradition" (παράδοσις). The term has several meanings, and hence the attitude of Christians toward "traditions" is ambivalent. The value of a "tradition"—in the realm of revealed truth —essentially depends on its "origin" (ἀρχή) and on its relation to this origin. There are merely human "traditions", of which God is not the "origin", even though they may be in a sense correct in their claim to rely on him—as in the case of divorce sanctioned by the Mosaic Law. ". . . But from the beginning [ἀπ ἀρχῆς] it was not so",[2] since God had originally joined man and woman in an inseparable unity.[3] Christ rejects such "human traditions", since they keep man from the actual will of God,[4] and the Lord came, after all, "to do his will",[5] namely, that genuine will of the Father which was "from the beginning", which has been obscured only because of sin and the Fall, with all of their consequences. It is in fact the distinguishing mark of the disciple of Christ that he does not abide by the "traditions of the elders" (see Mt 15:2).

It is an entirely different matter with the traditions about

[2] Mt 19:8.
[3] Gen 2:24.
[4] Mt 15:1−20.
[5] Cf. Jn 4:34.

"what was from the beginning", namely, the "old command-ment which you had from the beginning",[6] ever since Christ gave it to his disciples. It was reliably "delivered to us by those who from the beginning were the eyewitnesses and ministers of the word",[7] that is, by the apostles, who from "the beginning of the gospel",[8] that is, the baptism of John[9] and the corresponding manifestation of Jesus as the Christ, "have been with [him]."[10]

These are the "traditions which you were taught" and which we are to "hold"[11] if we are not to lose our asso-ciation with the "beginning" itself. Therefore, even if it were brought by "an angel from heaven", there cannot be "another gospel"[12] besides the one that was preached to us from the beginning, because it would not be the *Evangelium Christi*.

By its very nature, genuine tradition means having and preserving *fellowship* with the "eyewitnesses and ministers of the word" and, through them, with him about whom they testify.

> *That which was from the beginning,*
> *which we have heard,*
> *which we have seen with our eyes,*
> *which we have looked upon and touched with our hands,*
> *concerning the word of life . . . ,*
> *we proclaim also to you,*
> *so that you may have fellowship with us;*

[6] Cf. 1 Jn 2:7.
[7] Lk 1:2.
[8] Mk 1:1.
[9] Acts 1:21f.
[10] Jn 15:27.
[11] 2 Thess 2:15; cf. 1 Cor 11:2.
[12] Gal 1:6ff.

and our fellowship is [fellowship]
with the Father and with his Son Jesus Christ.[13]

This "fellowship" (κοινωνία) of believers among themselves and with God is what Scripture calls "Church" and "Body of Christ". It embraces *all* "members" of this Body, the living and also those who have already "died in the Lord". For the members are bound to one another and to the Body so closely that those who have died are not "dead members", since "all live to God".[14]

Whoever wants to have "fellowship with God", therefore, can never disregard those before him who were made worthy of this fellowship! In his response of faith to their "proclamation", the one who was born afterward enters into that selfsame fellowship of which those "eyewitnesses and ministers of the word" were "from the beginning" and forever remain a living part. Hence only that church is genuinely "Christ's Church" which stands in an unbroken, living fellowship with the apostles, upon whom the Lord, indeed, founded his Church.[15]

∼

What is said here about holding fast to "the good thing committed to thy trust",[16] that is, the apostolic tradition as it is set down in the writings of the apostles, is also true in an analogous way of those "original, unwritten traditions",[17]

[13] 1 Jn 1:1–4.
[14] Lk 20:38.
[15] Eph 2:20.
[16] 2 Tim 1:14.
[17] Evagrius, *Mal. cog.* 33, 28 (Paul Géhin, Claire Guillaumont, and Antoine Guillaumont [hereafter Géhin-Guillaumont]; PG 40, 1240 D).

which, though not contained explicitly in these apostolic testimonies, are still no less apostolic in their origins. For whether they are "written" or "unwritten", "with regard to piety, both have the same force."[18]

Both forms of apostolic tradition possess what one could call the "grace of the origin", since it was in them that the deposit entrusted to us at the beginning took shape. We will see farther on what this "unwritten tradition" comprises in particular. Here we want to ask first how the Fathers themselves understood their faithfulness with regard to the "origin".

$\sim$

The same attitude that Basil the Great exhibits toward the Church's tradition is to be found in his disciple Evagrius Ponticus with regard to the *spiritual tradition of monasticism*. This is how he writes to the monk Eulogios, for whom he wishes to explain several questions about the spiritual life:

"Not because of deeds done by us in righteousness"[19] *did we attain this, but rather because we have "the pattern of sound words"*[20] *which we have heard from the Fathers, and because we have become witnesses to some of their deeds.*

Everything, though, is a grace from above, which points out even to sinners the schemes of the tempter, and which also says for our safety, "What have you, then, that you did not receive?"— in order that we, in receiving, might thank the Giver, so as not to give ourselves the praise and the honor and thus deny the gift. Therefore grace says: "If then you received it, why do you boast as if it were not a gift? Already you have become rich," it says,

---

[18] Basil, *De Spiritu Sancto* XXVII, 66, 4–5 (Pruche).
[19] Tit 3:5.
[20] 2 Tim 1:13.

you who dispense with works; already you, who have begun to
teach, "are filled."[21]

Hence an initial reason not to put oneself forward as a
"teacher" is the humble acknowledgment of the elementary
fact that we are all *receivers*. The "Fathers" whom Evagrius
refers to here are, among others, his own masters and teachers, Macarius the Great and his namesake from Alexandria,
through whom he was connected with the "first of the anchorites", Anthony the Great, and thus with the origin of
monasticism itself. In another passage Evagrius elaborates
further on the thought.

> *It is also necessary to ask about the ways of those monks who*
> *went before us in an upright manner, and to be guided by them.*
> *For we find much that was beautifully said and done by them.*[22]

The "pattern of sound words" of the Fathers and their
"splendid deeds" are thus an *example*—the Greek word
(ὑποτύπωσις) translated as "pattern" can mean this, too—by
which one must be guided! This is precisely the reason why
the "words and deeds of the Fathers" were not only gathered
very early on, but were also quoted again and again. Benedict
of Nursia in the West is no different in his thinking when,
beyond his own "rules for beginners", he expressly refers
to the *doctrinae sanctorum Patrum* as an obligatory guideline
for all who are striving for perfection.[23]

Thus, for a Christian, the study of the holy Fathers can
never remain merely academic patrology, which does not
necessarily influence the life of the one who is studying.
The example of the holy Fathers, their words, and deeds are

---

[21] Evagrius, *De Vitiis* 1 (PG 79, 1140 B–C); quoting 1 Cor 4:7–8.
[22] Evagrius, *Praktikos* 91.
[23] *Regula Benedicti* 73, 2.

rather *a model that obliges one to imitate them*. Evagrius is not remiss in providing us with a justification for this statement.

It is fitting for those who want to walk along the "way" of him who said: "I am the way and the life,"[24] *that they learn from those who previously walked along it, and converse with them about what is useful, and hear from them what is helpful, so as not to introduce anything that is foreign to our course.*[25]

Not to be guided by the example of the holy Fathers and to want to go one's own way, therefore, involves the danger of "introducing something that is foreign to our course", that is, things "that are absolutely alien to monastic life"[26] because they have not been "tested" and found to be "good" by the "brothers" "who went before us in an upright manner".[27] Whoever has strayed thus from that "way" of the Fathers runs the risk of becoming himself "a stranger to our Savior's ways"[28] and thereby of estranging himself from the Lord, the "Way" par excellence!

The reference to what "the brothers have proved to be the best of all" already makes clear that by no means everything the Fathers did needs to be imitated, no matter how "splendid" it might be, and even if the Father in question were Anthony the Great himself. Let no one dare to imitate in every detail his extreme form of anchorite life, for instance, unless he wants to become the laughing-stock of the demons.[29] The Fathers themselves could distinguish very well between a "personal charism" and "tradition".

[24] Jn 14:6.

[25] Evagrius, *Epistula* 17, 1.

[26] Evagrius, *Antirrheticus* I, 27 (Frankenberg).

[27] Evagrius, *Mal. cog.* 35, 13–14 (Géhin-Guillaumont; PG 79, 1229 C).

[28] Ibid., 13, 3–4 (Géhin-Guillaumont; PG 79, 1216 C).

[29] Ibid., 35, 24–30 (Géhin-Guillaumont; PG 79, 1229 D).

~

The meaning and purpose of preserving the "tradition" is, then, for the Fathers, just as it was for the first "eyewitnesses and ministers of the word", *not an unthinking adherence to what has been handed down, but the preservation of a living fellowship.* Whoever wants to have fellowship with the Father can attain this only by "way" of the Son. One reaches the Son, though, only by way of "those who walked before us along the way" and thereby became themselves a living part of the "Way". These are, first of all, the apostles as the immediate "eyewitnesses of the Word". John writes very definitely, "So that *you* may have fellowship with *us*", and Evagrius aptly calls that "way" of *praktike* (ascetic struggle), which he has received from the Fathers, precisely "the apostolic way".[30] Hence all those Fathers in faith "who went before us in an upright manner" are "Way". Only the one who follows in their "footsteps" himself may hope to reach the destination of this way, as they did.[31]

It is therefore not enough just to call upon the "spirit of the Fathers"—which is difficult to define—or merely to "speak with pleasure about their deeds" at every opportunity, while leaving everything at the status quo. One must also strive to accomplish these deeds, even "amid great labors",[32] if one wants to have part in their fellowship.

Only in light of this does the title "first (ἀπαρχή) of the anchorites",[33] which Evagrius bestows on the "righteous Anthony",[34] acquire its full significance. Anthony the Great

---

[30] Evagrius, *Epistula* 25, 3.
[31] Cf. Evagrius, *Praktikos*, prol. [9].
[32] Evagrius, *Ad Eulogium* 16 (PG 79, 1113 B).
[33] Evagrius, *Mal. cog.* 35, 27 (Géhin-Guillaumont; PG 79, 1229 D).
[34] Evagrius, *Praktikos* 92.

is of course temporally the first anchorite, but that would mean nothing further were he not also the "first fruit". For the "first fruit", being "holy", "makes the entire lump of dough holy", just as the "holy root makes the branches holy"[35]—as long as they remain in living fellowship with it. The "beginning", because it is determined by the Lord himself, possesses in fact a special grace, namely, the "grace of the origin," of the "principle", which does not merely stand at the beginning temporally, but rather stamps with the seal of *authenticity* everything that remains *in living fellowship* with it.

∼

By adhering to the living fellowship with "what was from the beginning", man, who is bound to space and time, enters into the mystery of the One who, free from these limitations, "is the same yesterday, today and for ever",[36] that is, of the Son, who is himself "in the beginning"[37] in the absolute sense. Beyond space and time, this fellowship creates *continuity* and *identity* in the midst of a world that is subject to constant change.

This remaining identically the same is something that neither individual believers nor the Church as a whole could ever accomplish on their own. Guarding "the good thing committed to our trust" is always the fruit of the working of "the Holy Spirit who dwells in us"[38] and there "bear[s] witness"[39] to the Son. He it is, also, who does not only

[35] Rom 11:16.
[36] Heb 13:8.
[37] Jn 1:1.
[38] 2 Tim 1:14.
[39] Jn 15:26.

"guide [us] into all the truth"[40] but also for ages to come causes the testimony of the Master himself to be recognized in the testimony of the disciples.[41]

> Blessed is the monk who keeps the commandments of the Lord, and holy is he who observes the words of his fathers.[42]

∽

2. "Spirituality" and "the spiritual life"

Prayer is part of what we describe in a general way with the term "spirituality"; indeed it is the most noble expression of the "spiritual life" (vita spiritualis). Therefore, it is worth investigating what is actually meant here by "spiritual".

∽

By "spirituality" (derived from spiritus = spirit) is generally understood in contemporary usage anything having to do with the "soul", the "interior life", and our "spiritual nature", as distinguished from what belongs to the material, corporeal realm. In theological language, "spirituality" is simply equated with "piety" [in the sense of "being devout"]. Hence one can speak of various "spiritualities", for instance, with regard to the different forms of devotion or of "mysticism" in the individual religious orders; in recent times we may even speak of a distinctively "lay spirituality". But even outside of Christianity there is talk of the different "spiritualities" of the great world religions.

The fact that the concept of "spirituality" is so vaguely defined has extremely negative consequences for the Christian

---

[40] Jn 16:13.
[41] Cf. Lk 10:16.
[42] Evagrius, Ad Monachos 92 (Gressmann).

understanding of "the spiritual life". For as a result, many other things appear to be "spiritual" that actually belong to an entirely different sphere. This becomes clear immediately when we turn to Scripture and, moreover, to the Fathers. For here the adjective "spiritual" (πνευματικός), in the connection that is of interest to us, refers unambiguously to the *Person* of the Holy Spirit!

∼

The "Holy Spirit", in the Old Covenant thought to be the impersonal "power" of God, is revealed in the New Covenant as that "other Paraclete" whom the Son, our true paraclete [παράκλητος (advocate, intercessor)] with the Father,[43] sent to his disciples after his glorification by the Father,[44] so that he might "be with [them] forever"[45] after his return to the Father, "teach [them] all things",[46] and "guide [them] into all the truth".[47]

The "spiritual man" (πνευματικός), therefore, is the one who, thanks to the Holy Spirit and "taught by the Spirit", is able to judge "spiritual things" (τὰ πνευματικά) "spiritually" (πνευματικῶς) and to discern them. This is, of course, in contrast to the sensual, "natural man" (ψυχικός), who can neither receive nor understand "the things of the Spirit of God", precisely because he does not possess the Spirit of God and the "wisdom of God" remains "folly" to him.[48]

Therefore "spiritual" always signifies, both here and in other contexts in Paul's writings, "endowed with the Spirit"

[43] 1 Jn 2:1.
[44] Jn 15:26; 20:22.
[45] Jn 14:16.
[46] Jn 14:26.
[47] Jn 16:13.
[48] 1 Cor 2:6–16.

—wrought or inspired by *the Holy Spirit*; it is by no means merely a decorative epithet!

∽

The Fathers adopted the Pauline distinction between "spiritual" (pneumatic [of the Spirit]) and "natural" (psychic [that is, of the unaided human soul]) and applied it to the "spiritual life"; we will return to it later. Whenever Evagrius, who always chooses his words well, calls something "spiritual", he means by this, as a rule, "wrought by the Spirit" or else "inspired by the Spirit". Thus "spiritual contemplation",[49] for example, which has as its object the "spiritual reasons" for things,[50] is called "spiritual" because the Holy Spirit is the Revealer of divine mysteries.[51] The virtues,[52] the foremost of which is love,[53] are likewise called "spiritual" because they are "fruits of the Holy Spirit",[54] who forms them in the baptized soul. The "spiritual teacher"[55] is so named because he, as a "spiritual father", has received the "charism of the Spirit"[56] and thus is someone "endowed by the Spirit" in the Pauline sense.

If "he who is united with the Lord becomes one spirit with him",[57] and David [according to the psalm verse] "clung to the Lord", then he became as a result one spirit [with him]. He calls "spirit",

---

[49] Evagrius, *Mal. cog.* 40, 7 (Géhin-Guillaumont; PG 40, 1244 B).
[50] Ibid., 8, 5 (Géhin-Guillaumont; PG 79, 1208 C).
[51] Evagrius, *In Ps.* 118:131 vθ.
[52] Evagrius, *De Oratione* 132.
[53] Ibid., 77.
[54] Gal 5:22f.; Evagrius, *In Ps.* 51:10 δff.
[55] Evagrius, *De Oratione* 139.
[56] Evagrius, *Epistula* 52, 7.
[57] 1 Cor 6:17.

though, the one who is "endowed with the Spirit",[58] *just as the
"love that is not boastful"*[59] *characterizes him who has love.*[60]

In this sense, *prayer*, too, which is after all the quintes-
sence of the "spiritual life", is very often called "spiritual"
(πνευματική).[61] For it takes place "in spirit and in truth",[62]
that is, "in the Holy Spirit and in the only-begotten Son"[63],
wherefore it is often called "true prayer" as well.[64] In this
regard it is incumbent upon the Holy Spirit to prepare the
way for this gift of the Father.[65] For we would not even
know how to pray as we ought[66] unless the Holy Spirit vis-
ited us in our "unknowing".[67]

> *The Holy Spirit, who "bears with us in our weakness",*[68] *visits
> us even when we are still impure. And when he finds the intellect
> simply praying to him and full of love for the truth, he comes upon
> it and destroys the entire phalanx of thoughts or imaginations that
> besiege it and urges it on to an ardent longing for spiritual prayer.*[69]

At the summit of the "spiritual life" this Holy Spirit determines what then happens—which can now be described
as "mystical"—to such an extent that a Syrian Father can
speak of the degree of "spiritualization", which might even
be called the degree of "spirituality", had this term not been
deprived of any concrete meaning.

[58] Cf. 1 Cor 2:15ff.
[59] 1 Cor 13:4.
[60] Evagrius, *In Ps. 62:9 γ.*
[61] Evagrius, *De Oratione* 28, 50, 63, 72, 101.
[62] Jn 4:23.
[63] Evagrius, *De Oratione* 59.
[64] Ibid., 41, 65, 76, 113.
[65] Ibid., 59.
[66] Cf. Rom 8:26.
[67] Evagrius, *De Oratione* 70.
[68] Rom 8:26.
[69] Evagrius, *De Oratione* 63.

As the target is to the arrows, so it is with the intellect at the place of spiritualization when it receives what is viewed in contemplation. For just as it does not depend on the target, which arrow it receives, but rather on the archer who shoots at it, in the same way it does not depend on the intellect either, when it has entered the place of spiritualization, what object it contemplates, but rather on the Spirit, who leads it. The intellect, in fact, has no more control over itself, as soon as it has entered the place of spiritualization, but rather it contemplates every object of contemplation that shows itself to it until it receives another one, and then it leaves off and turns its attention away from the first. [70]

～

However much we may talk of "spirituality" and however fond we may be of using the epithet "spiritual", the *Person* of the Holy Spirit is the Great Absent One in the "spirituality" of the West, as has often been lamented. As a consequence, we regard many things as "spiritual" that in fact still belong absolutely and entirely to the realm of the "natural man", who is lacking precisely in the "gift of the Spirit". We mean here everything that falls within the scope of the "feelings" and "emotions", which are of a thoroughly irrational nature and are by no means "spiritual" or wrought by the Spirit.

Evagrius in fact distinguishes, as other Fathers also do, between a "rational", logos-endowed part of the soul (λογιστικόν μέρος) and an "irrational" part (ἄλογον μέρος). [71] The latter consists in turn of "desires" (ἐπιθυμητικόν) and "aggression" (θυμικόν) in Western terms, the "concupiscible" and "irascible" appetites of the soul, which taken together are also called the "passionate part" (παθητικόν μέρος) of the soul, [72] because through these two "powers", by means of

[70] Joseph Hazzaya (Joseph the Visionary), p. 190.
[71] Evagrius, *Praktikos* 66, 89.
[72] Evagrius, *In Ps.* 25:2 α.

which we deal with the world of the senses, the "irrational" passions make their way into the soul and then perplex and blind the "rational part".

Prayer, now, belongs entirely to this "rational part" of the soul; indeed it is "the preeminent and most authentic use of the intellect"![73] Prayer is not a matter of "feeling" and certainly not one of "sentimentality"—which is not to say that it consists of a purely "intellectual act" in the modern sense of the word. For "intellect" (νοῦς) is not identical with "understanding", but is rather to be rendered by "core of being", "person", or, in biblical terms, "the inner man".[74] Besides, Evagrius is very well acquainted with a "feeling of prayer",[75] as we will see farther on.

For now let the observation suffice that we would do well to distinguish carefully, with the Fathers, between that which is really "spiritual", namely, what is wrought by the Person of the Holy Spirit, and all that belongs to the domain of the "natural man", that is, our irrational wishes and desires. For the latter are, at best, indifferent in value; most often, though, they are the expression of our "self-love" (φι-λαυτία), which is the exact opposite of a "friendly love for God" (πρὸς θεὸν φιλία), in other words, that "perfect and spiritual love in which prayer acts in spirit and in truth".[76]

∼

3. "Action" and "contemplation"

The distinction between a "practical" (or "active") and a "theoretical" (or "contemplative") life is very old; it has

[73] Evagrius, De Oratione 84.
[74] Cf. Gabriel Bunge, "Nach dem Intellekt leben", in Simandron—Der Wachklopfer: Gedenkschrift Gamber (Cologne, 1989), pp. 95–109.
[75] Evagrius, De Oratione 43.
[76] Ibid., 77.

pre-Christian origins. The holy Fathers have adopted it, yet
in doing so they have filled both concepts with a new, specifically Christian content. Now they form the two pillars of
the spiritual life and, thus, of prayer as well. As happens so
often, though, shifts of meaning have crept in here as well,
particularly in the West, as a look at our colloquial usage
demonstrates.

"Theory" and "practice"—in that order!—are considered nowadays as two completely different things. People
like to contrast the "theoretician" wrapped up in his own
ideas with the sober "practitioner". Many things are dismissed as mere "theorizing", which carries no weight compared with "practical experience". In our everyday language,
to put it bluntly, "theory" is to "practice" approximately as
untested conjecture is to certain knowledge.

There probably would have been no end to the wonder-
ment of the Fathers at such a transposition of values, that
is, the complete misunderstanding of what "practice" and
"theory"—in that order!—really are, essentially and in relation to each other.

> *"The Lord loves the gates of Zion more than all the tents of Ja-
> cob":*
>
> *The Lord loves both the* praktikos *and also the* theoretikos.
> *More than the former, nevertheless, he loves the* theoretikos. *For
> Jacob [who symbolizes the practical man]*[77] *means "takes by the
> heel",*[78] *whereas Zion [which here symbolizes the contemplative
> intellect]*[79] *is translated as "observation post".*[80]

∽

[77] Cf. Evagrius, *In Ps.* 77:21 η.
[78] Gen 25:26.
[79] Evagrius, *In Ps.* 149:2 α.
[80] Ibid., 86:2 α.

Action and contemplation, the two Latin expressions corresponding to these Greek terms, have not fared much better,
either. The shifts in meaning and valuation that have oc-
curred in this regard could very well be responsible for the
reversal and revaluation of "practice" and "theory", also.
They go to the very roots of our modern understanding of
ourselves and hence have an immediate effect on our understanding of the spiritual life as well.

An "active life"—in the spiritual sense—is probably understood by most people today to be a life of "active" love
of neighbor, that is, one of charitable deeds. When the original religious motivation is gone, it becomes mere "social
activism".

In contrast to this "active life", there is the "contemplative life", as it is practiced by the so-called "contemplative
orders" in the seclusion of their cloisters—a life, it is generally thought, which is reserved for only a few. Such a
life consists, then, of contemplating (from *contemplatio*) the
things of God. Prayer is regarded as the first and greatest
occupation of these contemplative orders.

Whereas the activity in the first-mentioned case is directed
outward, toward one's neighbor, in the second case it is essentially inward activity. Therefore it is understandable that
the valuations usually assigned today to these forms of life
blatantly contradict the text by Evagrius cited above, which
unequivocally gives precedence to the "theoretician" (the
contemplative). Most people have the notion that the so-
called "active orders" are far more "useful" than the purely
"contemplative" communities. The former, in fact, are often
spared when hostile measures are taken against the Church,
while the contemplative orders are suppressed with no com-
punction as being (socially) "useless".

In recent times, of course, a new reevaluation of these two

forms of life is taking place to some extent. Since activity easily deteriorates into "activism", which ultimately leaves people empty, more and more lay people and religious are turning to various forms of "meditation", and not a few of them even dedicate all of their available time to "contemplation".

~

As we have said, it would have struck the Fathers as very strange if someone had spoken to them in this way about "theory" and "practice", the "active" and the "contemplative" life. Certainly, they, too, made a clear-cut distinction between a *praktikos* and a *theoretikos*. For instance, the two types are exposed to entirely different temptations and have different battles to fight. While the former has to deal first and foremost with the passions, the latter has to deal chiefly with errors in the realm of knowledge.[81] Hence the former fights his opponents by means of the virtues, whereas the latter, "making use of the doctrine of the truth, tears down every high building that is set up contrary to the knowledge of God".[82] Then, too, God loves the latter more than the former, as we have seen, since the one dwells already in God's own house, whereas the other still abides in the outer courts of it.[83]

Notwithstanding that, the *Church* nevertheless is made up of both "practitioners" and "theoreticians".[84] Indeed, it is not at all a question of two different subjects, and consequently there are not two different "ways", either, between which one could be free to choose arbitrarily or according

[81] Ibid., 143:7 ε.
[82] Ibid., 26:3 βb, citing 2 Cor 10:5.
[83] Ibid., 133:1 α.
[84] Ibid., 150:4b ξ.

to one's inclination. Rather, it is a matter of *one and the same person*, who, however, may find himself at *different stages* of one and the same spiritual way.[85] The *praktikos* is to the *theoretikos* in fact as Jacob is to Israel,[86] and these are indeed one and the same person. Jacob, the *praktikos*,[87] after he has wrestled with the angel and seen God face to face,[88] becomes Israel, the *theoretikos* (seer).[89]

~

It is the same thing, naturally, with *prayer*, too. Like everything else, it has two sides or aspects. In contrast to the "practical manner", there is the "theoretical" (contemplative) manner, and one is related to the other as "the letter" is to "the spirit", whereby the spirit naturally precedes the letter and endows it with "meaning". The two "manners" are, therefore, inseparable from each other! Likewise it is one and the same Jacob who first serves for seven years to win the unloved "Leah", symbol of the laborious "active manner", and then works seven more years to win the beloved "Rachel", symbol of contemplation.[90]

Since the "theoretical manner" of prayer, then, consists of contemplation of the triune God and of his creation, something also called "*theologike*" and "*physike*" [φυσική, that is, knowledge about the natures of things], what are we to understand by the "practical manner" of prayer? The latter is a part of what Evagrius calls "*praktike*" [ἐ πρακτική] and

---

[85] Ibid., 117:10 β.
[86] Ibid., 77:21 η.
[87] Cf. Evagrius, *De Oratione*, prol.
[88] Gen 32.
[89] Cf. Eusebius, *Praeparatio Evangelica* VII, 9, 28 (Mras).
[90] Evagrius, *De Oratione*, prol.

defines as follows: The *praktike* is a spiritual method that completely cleanses the passionate part of the soul.[91]

This "spiritual method" consists essentially of "keeping the commandments",[92] an endeavor assisted by all those practices that we designate as "ascetical" in the widest sense. Their goal is, with God's help, to restore to the soul its natural "health,"[93] which consists of "apatheia", freedom from the "sicknesses" (or passions—πάθη) that estrange it from God. Without this dispassionate character, which is attained by degrees,[94] the spiritual life (and prayer with it) deteriorates into *self-deception*, and that removes man even farther from God.

> *Just as it is of no benefit to someone whose eyes are diseased to look uninterruptedly into the full glare of the burning noonday sun without covering them, so too it is of no use whatsoever for the passionate and impure intellect to imitate the surpassing prayer in spirit and in truth, which calls for reverence. On the contrary, he will instead provoke the Deity to displeasure with him!*[95]

"Bewildered" and "blinded" by his passions,[96] through such "defeats" many a man even runs the risk of becoming ultimately a "source of lying doctrines and opinions"[97], thus not only deceiving himself, but also leading others astray.

~

[91] Evagrius, *Praktikos* 78.
[92] Ibid., 81.
[93] Ibid., 56.
[94] Ibid., 60.
[95] Evagrius, *De Oratione* 146.
[96] Evagrius, *Kephalaia Gnostika* V, 27 (Guillaumont).
[97] Ibid., V, 38.

The "active life" as understood by the Fathers, then, certainly does include an *activity* (praxis), but one that is not just outwardly directed; this activity makes no distinction at all between "interior" and "exterior". *Praktike*, rather, embraces the entire realm of relations that a human being has to himself, to his neighbor, and to things; it is therefore called "ethics" as well.[98]

Praktike and *theoretike* are not two mutually independent "paths", but rather the two great stages of one and the same path. *Theoria* (contemplation) is the natural "horizon" of *praxis*, which leads step by step to the former, its goal, toward which it is aimed and from which alone it receives its reason for being.

> *These are the words that the Fathers constantly repeat [to their*
>   *spiritual sons]:*
> *Faith, children, is made firm by the fear of God,*
> *and this in turn is guaranteed by continence;*
> *the latter, though, is made unbending by patience and hope,*
> *from which the absence of passions is born,*
> *while the shoot that springs from this is love.*
> *Love, however, is the gate to natural knowledge [that is,*
>   *knowledge of the natures of things],*
> *which is followed by theology [the knowledge of God] and the*
>   *final beatitude.*[99]

All of those (apparently) "external aspects" of prayer, to which in the following pages such great significance will be attributed, belong jointly and severally to "the practical manner of prayer", although, being what they are, they already contain within themselves their goal, "the contemplative manner", as their natural horizon. As is true of the

[98] Evagrius, *In Ps. 143:1* α.
[99] Evagrius, *Praktikos*, prol. [8].

practike in general, they are bound up with difficulties, just like the life of constant self-denial that Jacob led for seven years as suitor of the beloved Rachel. And yet this is not a matter of a "self-redemption", however that may be understood! For the goal of *praktike*—"purity of heart", which alone enables a human being to "see God"[100]—is always the fruit of the *cooperation* of "God's grace and human effort,"[101] in that order! The "contemplative manner of prayer" itself is then, just like *theoria* in general, a "charism",[102] pure and simple, a "gift" of the Father[103] to those whom he has found worthy of it.[104]

~

4. "Psalmody"—"Prayer"—"Meditation"

Not infrequently today one meets people, even clerics, who declare outright that they are not going to "pray" any more, but instead will only "meditate". A wealth of publications on the theme of "meditation", courses of instruction, and the like show that a crisis in "prayer" has evidently developed among Christians. The situation is somewhat better with psalmody, or "praying the psalms", as people like to say, which even today is carried on principally by the religious orders, but which also forms the centerpiece of the "Liturgy of the Hours" belonging to the entire Church, both laity and clergy.

Psalmody, prayer, and meditation have been a regular component of the spiritual life of the "biblical man" from time

---

[100] Mt 5:8.
[101] Evagrius, *In Ps. 17:21* ιβ.
[102] Evagrius, *De Oratione* 87.
[103] Ibid., 59, 70.
[104] Evagrius, *In Ps. 13:7* ξ and frequently.

immemorial. But what does tradition understand by this? Let us begin with psalmody and prayer.

∿

If you have not yet received the charism of prayer or of psalmody, then [ask] perseveringly, and you will receive![105]

The *distinction* between psalmody and prayer that is evidently presupposed here and which is a matter of course in the writings of the early Fathers, appears strange to the modern reader. Are not psalmody and prayer one and the same, so that one can rightly speak of the "prayer from psalms" or of "praying the psalms"? And is not the Psalter *the* "prayer book of the Church", which took it over from the synagogue? The Fathers would have answered: Yes and no. "Psalmody is *not yet* praying", for the two belong to different (not separate) orders.

Psalmody belongs to [the realm of] "manifold wisdom",[106] *whereas prayer is the prelude to immaterial knowledge, which is not manifold.*[107]

How is this to be understood? Let us look first at what Scripture, in particular the Psalter, itself says about psalmody and prayer.

∿

A "psalm" is a "song" that, as such, can have the most varied contents. Bible scholarship in fact has assigned the 150 psalms to various literary genres. Such a "song" in the

[105] Evagrius, *De Oratione* 87.
[106] Eph 3:10.
[107] Evagrius, *De Oratione* 85.

Old Covenant, as is still evident from many psalm titles, was often performed with musical accompaniment, for instance using the ten-stringed "psaltery". This performance was called "psalmody", and the artist himself a "psaltode" (cf. "rhapsode") or psaltes, that is, a singer of psalms. Collected in five books, these "songs of Israel" were adopted from the people of the Old Covenant by the early Church and in the course of time were made a permanent part of her own divine worship. She has her own manner, however, of reading this "Book of Psalms".

It would not be wrong to call the Psalter a summary of the entire Scripture of the Old Covenant in the form of hymns. Therefore, from the very beginning, the Church has read the Psalms, as she has generally read the books of the Old Testament, as a *prophetic word* of the Holy Spirit pointing to fulfillment in Christ.[108] This already explains in part what Evagrius means when he assigns psalmody to the realm of the "manifold wisdom of God" and thus regards it as a testimony to that "wisdom" which is reflected in creation and in the history of salvation, to which the Scriptures of the Old Covenant as a whole bear witness.

For Christians, then, the Psalter is first of all *Scripture*, and its author, David, is a prophet. As a prophetic *word of God to man* that opens a prospect on to Christ and his Church, it is constantly cited in the New Testament as well, more than any other book of the Old Testament.

"Prayer", on the other hand, and also the singing of "hymns" of "praise" (δοξολογία), is *man's speaking to God* or, according to the definition of Clement of Alexandria, a

---

[108] Cf. Lk 24:44.

"dialogue with God".[109] The Psalter offers not a few examples of this "speaking to God" and also of "hymns of praise" that the praying Christian can immediately make his own. Extensive passages of the Psalter, however, do not have the form of a prayer at all. Beside long reflections on the changeable history of Israel, we even find not a few psalms (or parts thereof) cursing the "enemies" in a way that appears to the modern reader as the exact opposite of Christian prayer! To be able to make the *entire* Psalter one's own and to transform it into genuinely *Christian* prayer—including those unpopular passages—requires zeal in practicing "meditation".

∼

By "meditation" (μελέτη) the Fathers (and the psalmist himself) understood a constant repetition of certain verses or entire passages of Sacred Scripture *sotto voce*[110] (in an undertone), with the goal of grasping their hidden *spiritual sense*. Hence Evagrius in one instance simply interprets "meditation" as "contemplation" (θεωρία).[111] Besides "meditating", Scripture therefore also speaks of "being mindful". Alluding to Psalm 137:1, Evagrius calls such contemplative "meditation" on the psalms "singing psalms to God in the sight of the angels", since the principal activity of the angels consists of contemplating God and his works.[112]

"I will sing praise to thee in the sight of the angels":
To sing psalms in the sight of the angels means to sing psalms

[109] Clement of Alexandria, *Stromata* VII, 39, 6.
[110] Cf. Ps 34:38; 36:30; 70:24.
[111] Evagrius, *In Ps. 118:92* μ α.
[112] Evagrius, *Kephalaia Gnostika* III, 4 (Guillaumont).

> *without distraction, whereby our intellect is either impressed only*
> *with the things described in the psalm or else receives no impres-*
> *sions.*
>
> *Or perhaps that person sings psalms "in the sight of the angels"*
> *who perceives the meaning of the psalms,*[113]

without allowing himself to become "distracted" by the va-
riety of images therein or by the multiplicity of concepts.
This is by no means easy, and for this reason Evagrius considers "psalmody without distraction" to be an even greater
thing than "praying without distraction",[114] since prayer,
as we saw earlier, is the "prelude to immaterial and non-
manifold knowledge" of the One God.

∼

The object of this "meditation" is God,[115] as he reveals
himself in his manifold "works"[116] from all eternity.[117]
These "works" testify to his "wisdom",[118] his "righteousness",[119] his "statutes"[120] and "ordinances",[121] which are
all the expression of that "manifold wisdom" of which Evagrius speaks.

[113] Evagrius, *In Ps. 137:1* α.
[114] Evagrius, *Praktikos* 69.
[115] Ps 62:7.
[116] Ps 67:12f.; 142:5.
[117] Ps 76:6.
[118] Ps 36:30.
[119] Ps 70:16, 24.
[120] Ps 118:16, 23, 48, 117.
[121] Ps 118:52.

The believer who prays finds these "testimonies"[122] set down in the "words" of God,[123] that is, in his "Law"[124] and his "commandments",[125] that is to say, in the Scriptures of the Old Covenant, which testify to his "wonderful works".[126]

Nevertheless, the hidden meaning of Scripture is disclosed to the praying Christian only when the Lord himself and his followers, the apostles and the Fathers, open his eyes to it.

> [Then the risen Lord] said to them: "These are my words which I spoke to you, while I was still with you, that everything written about me in the law of Moses and the prophets and the psalms must be fulfilled." Then he opened their minds to understand the scriptures, and said to them, "Thus it is written, that the Christ should suffer and on the third day rise from the dead, and that repentance and forgiveness of sins should be preached in his name to all nations, beginning from Jerusalem. You are witnesses of these things."[127]

~

Biblical "meditation", then, has to do mainly with the objective facts of salvation history, in which God reveals himself, his "Name".[128] "Reflection" upon the enigmatic history of the Chosen People[129] or on one's own destiny, in which this history is repeated, is thus never an end in itself, but

[122] Ps 118:24, 99.
[123] Ps 118:148.
[124] Ps 1:2; 118:70, 77, 92, 97.
[125] Ps 118:15, 47, 78, 143.
[126] Ps 104:5; 118:27.
[127] Lk 24:44–48.
[128] Ps 118:55.
[129] Ps 77.

should always lead to "being mindful" of God[130] himself, and thus also to "prayer" in the strict sense. For in prayer, man *responds* to this salvific action of God, whether it be in petitions, hymns, or praise.

> *"My lips will pour forth praise when thou dost teach me thy statutes":*
>
> *Just as singing psalms is fitting for the cheerful man—"Is any one among you cheerful? Let him sing praise", it says*[131] *—likewise singing hymns is fitting for those who see the reasons for the "statutes".*
>
> *Nonetheless singing psalms is suited to men, whereas singing hymns is suited to the angels, or else to those who possess an almost angelic state. Thus the shepherds who were spending the night out in the open heard the angels singing, not psalms, but hymns, and saying, "Glory to God in the highest, and peace on earth, among men of goodwill."*[132]
>
> *"Cheerfulness", then, consists in the dispassionate quality of the soul, which is attained through [keeping] the commandments of God and through the true teachings; a "hymn", in contrast, is a song of praise associated with wonder and astonishment at the sight of the things that God has accomplished.*[133]

∼

For the holy Fathers, therefore, "psalmody", "prayer", and "meditation" were quite different though intimately interwoven things.

---

[130] Ps 62:7; 76:4.
[131] Jas 5:13.
[132] Lk 2:14.
[133] Evagrius, *In Ps. 118:171* οθ.

It was said of Ioannes Kolobos that, when he returned from the harvest or from a visit of the elder Fathers, he dedicated himself to prayer, meditation, and psalmody, until his thinking had again attained its original order.[134]

If one were to take to heart again this distinction, which presents an abundance of food for thought, then quite a few of the problems that many people have today with psalmody —which is still the heart of the Liturgy of the Hours— would vanish. Psalmody is first of all reading Scripture, even though in this case "Scripture" and "reading" are of a very particular sort. The psalm is an *Old Testament* word of God, which one must in the first place accept as such, and that means *in its entirety* and unadulterated, together with all those parts that are offensive to contemporary sensibilities.

The "spiritualization" of this Old Testament word of God —*in the Holy Spirit* opening its horizons toward Christ and his Church—must not be done through toned-down translations and certainly not, as has become the custom today, through omissions! Only inspired "meditation" is capable of accomplishing this "spiritualization", which is of course necessary for the Scriptures of the Old Testament in general. The Christian finds the key to such an opening up toward Christ and his Church in the "typological" manner in which the New Testament—and subsequently the Fathers of the Church—read the Old Testament word of God.

In the personal "prayer", which originally followed each psalm in the Liturgy of the Hours,[135] the circle is then completed, in that man now turns in intimate "conversation"

---

[134] Joannes Kolobos 35.
[135] See below, page 108.

to him who, through countless generations and the vicissitudes of history, despite human tragedies and sinful failures, has brought his work of salvation to perfection at last in Christ.

～

Chapter II

Places and Times

"Praying" is by its very essence something that takes place spiritually between God and man, and our "intellect", having a spiritual nature, would be capable of praying by itself, without the body, as Evagrius assures us.[1] Nevertheless, the human being consists of soul and body, and since the latter is tied up with space and time, human prayer in fact always occurs in space and time also. Choosing a suitable place and setting aside the most appropriate hours of the day or night are therefore by no means inessential prerequisites for what the Fathers call "true prayer".

Among the things necessary for prayer, Origen, having spoken about the inner disposition of the one who prays, includes "place", "orientation", and "time", too. We, too, wish to keep to this sequence.

1. *"When you pray, go into your room"* (Mt 6:6)

For many Christians today, the only definition of "prayer" left is: participating in a liturgy or public devotions. Personal prayer has disappeared to a great extent or has yielded its place to the various forms of "meditation". For the man of biblical times and for the Fathers, in contrast, it was self-evident that one not only participated regularly and at fixed

[1] Evagrius, *Praktikos* 49.

times in the common prayer of all the faithful, but, in addition to that, also withdrew, just as regularly, for personal prayer.

In the earthly deeds of Jesus Christ, Christians in every age have seen an example and a guide. Thus we hear that our Lord regularly participated in the Sabbath celebrations in the synagogues of Palestine, and also that even as a child he would go on pilgrimage to Jerusalem for the great feasts. In a similar way, every pious Jew of that time probably kept these customs. What seems to have impressed his disciples in particular, though, and what they have consequently recorded over and over again for us, was his altogether personal prayer.

Evidently Christ had the habit of regularly praying "alone".[2] For this utterly personal conversation with his Heavenly Father, he preferred to withdraw "to a lonely place" or to "a wilderness"[3] or "into the hills by himself".[4] Thus, when he wanted to pray, he regularly withdrew from the crowd, to whom he knew that he had been sent,[5] and even from his disciples,[6] who otherwise accompanied him constantly. Even in the Garden of Gethsemane, where he had expressly brought them along, he left behind his most intimate confidants, Peter and the two sons of Zebedee, and went on farther about the distance of "a stone's throw"— hence out of earshot—so as to be all alone in prayer and to commend his soul, which was sorrowful unto death, to the will of his Father.[7]

What he himself did during his earthly life he also taught

[2] Lk 9:18.
[3] Mk 1:35; Lk 5:16.
[4] Mt 14:23; cf. Mk 6:46; Lk 6:12; 9:28.
[5] Cf. Mk 1:38.
[6] Mk 1:36f.
[7] Lk 22:41 and parallel passages.

his disciples explicitly. Contrary to a widespread pious custom of standing in the public places and on the street corners
to pray whenever the sound of the trumpet announced the
beginning of the morning and evening sacrifice in the temple, Christ commands his followers to withdraw into the
most secret "room" of their own house for prayer, where
only the "Father who is in secret" can see and hear.[8]

～

The apostles and, after them, the holy Fathers did just that.
We see Peter and John "going up to the temple at the hour
of prayer, the ninth hour",[9] and how the entire early Church
"devoted themselves to prayer",[10] but also how Peter, alone,
"went up on the housetop to pray, [at] about the sixth
hour".[11] As we see, one can pray in any place, wherever
one happens to be. Nonetheless, if someone wants to devote himself to personal prayer, he will look for an appropriate place. Peter was on a journey, and in order to be alone
he had no other choice than the flat roof of the house in
which he was a guest.

In a time when it still went without saying that a Christian would regularly pray each day, the Fathers deal also with
the question of the suitable place for this personal prayer.

> *About the place [for prayer] one should know that, provided one
> prays correctly, every place is appropriate for prayer. For "in every
> place, says the LORD, incense is offered to my name,"[12] and: "I
> desire then that in every place the men should pray."[13]*

[8] Mt 6:5-6.
[9] Acts 3:1.
[10] Acts 1:14 and passim.
[11] Acts 10:9.
[12] Mal 1:11.
[13] 1 Tim 2:8.

> *Still, in order that each person may say his prayers in peace
> and without distraction, there is also a command to select in one's
> own house if possible the so-called holiest place and . . . to pray
> [there].*[14]

The first Christians, in fact, and the early monks in the
Egyptian desert also, reserved whenever possible a particular
room of their house that was quiet and oriented in a particular way for the recitation of their private prayers. The
oratories of the early Egyptian Desert Fathers, which in the
past few decades have emerged again from the sand, are
easily recognized as such. Of course that did not prevent
Christians from being partial to praying in places "where
the faithful gather, as it is natural to do", Origen continues,

> *since [in such places] both angelic powers stand beside the masses
> of the faithful and also "the power of our Lord"*[15] *and Savior
> himself, furthermore also the spirits of the saints, and even, as I
> believe, those of the recently departed, but clearly also [the spirits]
> of those who are still alive, even though it is not easy to explain
> "how".*[16]

This magnificent testimony to a powerful, living awareness of what we call "the communion of saints", but are
now able to experience only with difficulty, dates from a
time when the Christians, as a persecuted faith community,
were not yet allowed to build "churches" in the strict sense
and had to gather in the halls of large private houses.

⁓

[14] Origen, *De Oratione* XXXI, 4.
[15] Cf. 1 Cor 5:4.
[16] Origen, *De Oratione* XXXI, 5.

The Fathers took very much to heart Christ's warning against that public display of one's own piety, that is, *hypocrisy*, that subtle vice of "pious" souls.

> *Vainglory recommends*
> *praying in the marketplaces,*
> *But whoever resists this,*
> *prays in his room.*[17]

We know from many reports that the Desert Fathers made every effort to carry out their ascetical practices—and particularly their prayers—in any event in secret. The example of Christ and also of many Fathers demonstrates, however, that it was not just a matter of avoiding sins of vanity. Prayer, after all, is by nature and most profoundly a "conversation of the mind with God", in which the presence of others can in some circumstances be a distraction.

> *Abba Markos spoke to Abba Arsenios: "Why do you flee from us?" Then the elder said to him: "God knows that I love you. But I cannot be with God and [at the same time] with men. The thousands and myriads [of angels] above have [but] one will;*[18] *men, though, have many wills. I cannot leave God and go among men."*[19]

Yet the danger of distraction through the presence of other people, which we must take into consideration in public prayer as well, is not the ultimate reason why those who truly pray long for solitude. During this "being with God" of which Arsenios spoke, things occur between Creator and creature that by their very nature are not meant for the eyes and ears of others.

[17] Evagrius, *De Octo Spiritibus Malitiae* VII, 12 (German translation); XVI (PG 79, 1161 A).

[18] Cf. Mt 6:10.

[19] Arsenios 13.

A brother went to the cell of Abba Arsenios at Scetis. He looked through the window and then saw the elder as if completely on fire. The brother, though, was worthy of seeing this. And when he knocked, the elder came out and saw the brother quite alarmed and said to him: "Have you been knocking for long? Have you perhaps seen something here?" And he replied, "No." And after speaking with him, he sent him away.[20]

This mysterious "incandescent prayer" is known to us from other Fathers also;[21] Evagrius speaks of it,[22] as does John Cassian.[23] The time for it is principally at night, when the visible world withdraws into darkness; the place for it is the barren "desert", the high "mountain" that separates us from everything, and when these are not accessible, then the hidden "room".

∼

2. *"Look toward the east, O Jerusalem!"* (Bar 4:36)

All of us are quite familiar with the term "orientation" from everyday language. Most people probably associate it only with the idea of being "aligned" in a particular way. Someone who "loses his orientation" has in fact lost sight of his direction and goal. Scarcely anyone realizes any more that "orientation" means, very precisely, "east-ing". "To orient oneself" means to turn toward the east, toward the *sunrise* (ἀνατολή).

Moreover, hardly anyone today besides the liturgists knows that all Christian churches are "easted", or at least in

---

[20] Arsenios 27.
[21] Isaiah 4; Joseph of Panepho 6, 7.
[22] Evagrius, *De Oratione* 111.
[23] Cassian, *Conlationes* IX, 15ff. (Petschenig).

principle should be orient-ed,[24] because Christians from time immemorial *used to turn to the east to pray.*

This turning toward the east in prayer is of such great importance in the eyes of the holy Fathers that it is worthwhile lingering a bit longer on this subject. Origen states it categorically: There is no reason that should ever prevent a Christian from turning toward the east to pray![25] The question as to "why" this orientation, is not a new one.

Question: *If God, the Lord of nature and of the universe, determined everything in creation according to the manner of the circle—wherefore David, too, has commanded us to "bless the LORD . . . in all places of his dominion",[26] and the Apostle has charged us to do the same, "in every place the men should pray, lifting holy hands [to God]"[27]—then why do we send hymns and prayers up to God while looking toward the sunrise, as though we considered that direction as an honorable work and as a divine dwelling place? And who taught the Christians this custom?*

Answer: *Since we usually appoint what is more honorable to the glory of God, and since according to men's way of thinking the sunrise is more honorable than the other directions in creation, therefore we all bow to the east when we pray. Just as we seal those persons who need it [with a blessing] in Christ's name using the right hand, because it is considered more honorable than the left hand, although it differs from the latter by convention and not by nature, even so the east, as the more honorable direction in creation, is appointed for the worship of God.*

Besides, the fact that we say our prayers facing toward the east in no way contradicts the word of the prophet or of the Apostle. For "in every place" the east is available for the one who prays. And since we worship [turned] in that direction in which we are facing,

---

[24] *Constitutiones Apostolicae* II, 57, 3 (Funk).

[25] Origen, *De Oratione* XXXI, 1.

[26] Ps 102:22.

[27] 1 Tim 2:8.

> *but it is impossible during prayer to look in all four directions of*
> *creation, therefore we perform our acts of worship while looking in*
> *one direction of creation: neither because it alone is God's work,*
> *nor because it has been designated the dwelling place of God, but*
> *because it has been designated the place of the worship that we*
> *offer to God.*
>
> *The Church, moreover, received the custom of praying from*
> *the same ones from whom she also received the custom of where*
> *to pray, that is, from the holy apostles.*[28]

The question raised here is legitimate enough. Certainly the Jews worship in Jerusalem and the Samaritans on the Garizim,[29] and whenever a pious Jew found himself away from the Holy City, he turned in prayer in the direction of Jerusalem, where God's temple stood.[30] Yet with the coming of Christ, this alignment *with a particular place* ceased in principle to apply. The "place" of the presence of God is Christ himself. The "true worshipers of the Father" worship him from now on "in spirit and truth".[31]

The unknown author of the *Answers* also states bluntly that the Christian custom (ἔθος) of bowing in prayer while turned toward the east, is based on a human convention (θέσει) and is not essential (φύσει). Why men—and in particular Christians—consider the "orient" as more honorable than the other three points of the compass he does not reveal to us; other Fathers, both earlier and later ones, give us detailed information on the subject. Of interest is the remark that we necessarily bow in the direction in which we are facing. Man has, in fact, a *face*, in the bodily as well as in

[28] Pseudo-Justin Martyr, *Quaestiones et responsiones ad orthodoxos*, question no. 118 (ΒΕΠ 4, pp. 129f.; PG 6:1368 B–D).

[29] Jn 4:20.

[30] Dan 6:10.

[31] Jn 4:23.

the spiritual sense, which he *turns* toward the one whom he wishes to address—a gesture of deep, symbolic significance, as everyone knows from experience.

Finally the author states also that the custom of turning toward the east in prayer is a matter of *apostolic tradition* and that this custom is therefore a fundamental part of the Church. This is the opinion of other Fathers as well, for instance Basil the Great.[32]

～

From apostolic times, then, Christians have turned in prayer toward the east and facing that direction have bowed in worship before God—not because they thought that God could only be seen there, as Gregory of Nyssa observes.[33] Why, then? Well, already in the fourth century that was not understood by all.

> *Therefore we all look to the east during prayer, but few know that we are in search of our original home, Paradise, which God planted in the Garden of Eden, to the east.*[34]

The first and most important reason why Christians consider the east as more honorable than the other three points of the compass and turn in that direction to pray is thus *a matter of salvation history*: the situation of Paradise "in the east".[35] Paradise is that place in which God's "original", initial, and most authentic will was realized in creation. The sin of the first human couple disturbed this order and led to their banishment from this "original home".[36] Nevertheless

---

[32] Basil the Great, *De Spiritu Sancto* XXVII, 66, 13f. (Pruche).
[33] Gregory of Nyssa, *De Oratione Dominica* 5 (PG 44, 1184).
[34] Basil the Great, *De Spiritu Sancto* XXVII, 66, 60f. (Pruche).
[35] Gen 2:8.
[36] Gen 3:23f.

this initial creative will of God remained in force. Therefore included already in the punishment was also the promise that this banishment would not be final.

> *Thus God "drove" Adam—and evidently his wife also—"out of Paradise". What was driven out, though, has an opportunity of returning. For God did not send him away without any hope of return, but rather since he was placed by God "over against" [Paradise],*[37] *he would live remembering it, having it plainly in view.*[38]

Christ's work of salvation consists in fulfilling this promise and thus validating again God's original will in creation. Hence he says, for instance in relation to divorce, which the Mosaic Law permitted: "[But] from the beginning it was not so!"[39] This "beginning" (ἀρχή)—not only in the temporal sense, but rather in the fundamental sense of "principle"—is and remains decisive. Therefore no man may put asunder what God "in the beginning" has joined together.[40] Thus says the WORD, because he himself, absolutely speaking, "was in the beginning with God"[41] and is perfectly one with God's initial and most characteristic will.

When the Christian, therefore, turns toward the east to worship, then in his mind's eye arises that Paradise as the "original home", where he is totally himself: living in perfect harmony with his Creator, with whom, indeed, he speaks there face to face, in harmony with his equals, with himself and with the creatures that surround him. He looks at the "tree of life", from which he is now no longer excluded

[37] Gen 3:24.
[38] Didymos, *In Gen VII*, 16, 9ff. (Nautin, p. 262).
[39] Mt 19:8.
[40] Mt 19:4–6.
[41] Jn 1:1.

thanks to Christ's death on the Cross—which is why the easterly direction for prayer has been marked with a cross on the wall from time immemorial. That explains why it is only this orientation in prayer that makes the praying Christian aware of the whole soteriological depth of the petition in the Our Father for the forgiveness of sins, as Gregory of Nyssa sets forth in a profound meditation.

> *When, therefore, we look [toward the East] in prayer and thought-fully call to mind the Fall from the bright, eastern places of blessed-ness, we fittingly attain an understanding of the word ["forgive us our debts, as we too forgive our debtors, and lead us not into temptation."]*[42]

~

These "debts", which we ourselves have incurred, are rooted in the original sin of Adam, from which only the Cross of Christ was able to deliver us.[43] This brings us to the second soteriological reason that the Fathers give for the ancient custom of praying while facing the east: the *saving work of Christ*, in which the original creative will of God becomes an eschatological reality. In his summary of the orthodox faith, John Damascene, the heir of a rich theological tradition, reviews the entire trajectory of salvation history.

> *It is not without reason or by chance that we worship toward the east. On the contrary, since we are composed of a visible and an invisible nature, of an intellectual nature and a sensitive one, that is, we also offer a two-fold worship to the Creator. It is just as we also sing both with our mind and with our bodily lips, and as we are baptized both in water and in the Spirit, and as we are united to the Lord in two ways when we receive the sacrament and the grace of the Spirit.*

[42] Gregory of Nyssa, *De Oratione Dominica* 5 (PG 44, 1184 BC).
[43] Col 2:14.

And so, since God is spiritual light[44] and Christ in sacred Scripture is called "Sun of Justice"[45] and "Orient,"[46] the East should be dedicated to His worship. For everything beautiful should be dedicated to God from whom everything that is good receives its goodness.

Also, the divine David says: "Sing to God, ye kingdoms of the earth: sing ye to the Lord; who mounteth above the heaven of heavens, to the east."[47] And still again, Scripture says: "And the Lord had planted a paradise in Eden to the east; wherein he placed man whom he had formed,"[48] and whom He cast out, when he had transgressed, "and made him to live over against the paradise of pleasure," or in the west.[49] Thus it is that, when we worship God, we long for our ancient fatherland and gaze toward it. The tabernacle of Moses had the veil and the propitiatory to the east;[50] and the tribe of Juda, as being the more honorable, pitched their tents on the east;[51] and in the celebrated temple of Solomon the gate of the Lord was set to the east.[52]

As a matter of fact, when the Lord was crucified, He looked toward the west,[53] and so we worship gazing towards Him. And

---

[44] 1 Jn 1:5.

[45] Mal 4:2.

[46] Zach 3:8; Lk 1:78.

[47] Ps 67:34.

[48] Gen 2:8.

[49] This is to be inferred from the Hebrew, not from the Greek text of Genesis 3:24.

[50] This follows from Lev 16:14.

[51] Num 2:3. From the tribe of Judah comes the Messiah!

[52] 1 Chron 9:18.

[53] Probably based on Lk 23:45: The sun was darkened to suggest that Christ, the "Sun of righteousness", the "Orient", faced the occident (the west) in death. Cf. Athanasius, *In Ps. 67:5* [= RSV Ps 68:4], where the words, "to him, who rides beyond the west" are interpreted as "to him, who descended into the nether world" (Athanasius) (PG 27, 293 B).

when He was taken up, He ascended to the east[54] and thus the
Apostles worshiped Him and thus He shall come in the same way
as they had seen Him going into heaven,[55] as the Lord Himself
said: "As lightning cometh out of the east and appeareth even into
the west: so shall also the coming of the Son of man be."[56] And
so, while we are awaiting Him, we worship toward the east.

This is, moreover, the unwritten tradition of the Apostles, for
they have handed many things down to us unwritten.[57]

What appears at first glance to be only a collection of
proof-texts for the unwritten apostolic custom of worshiping toward the east proves upon closer inspection to be a
coherent theological treatment of the subject.

John Damascene begins with a general statement: the
twofold, corporal-sensual and rational-spiritual nature of man
demands also a *twofold worship*. The thought probably is taken
from Origen: the inner, spiritual attitude in prayer demands,
sensibly enough, an expression suited to it in the attitude of
the person praying.[58] When the Christian who is worshiping in the spirit *turns* to the Lord, this must be manifested
also in the body in a corresponding way.

[54] Cf. Athanasius, *In Ps. 67:34* (PG 27, 303 CD): "Since in the preceding (i.e., in verse 5) he announced the suffering of Christ and his
descent to the nether world, therefore he also announces his ascension
into heaven. The words 'toward the east', though, are by way of analogy. For as the sun climbs up from the sunset to the sunrise, in the
same way, too, the Lord lifted himself as though from the depths of
the nether world to the heaven of heavens." Cf. also Evagrius, *In Ps.
67:34 xa* (with reference to Eph 4:10).

[55] Acts 1:11.

[56] Mt 24:27.

[57] John Damascene, *De Fide Orthodoxa (On the Orthodox Faith)* IV, 12
(English translation: St. John of Damascus, *Writings*, trans. Frederic H.
Chase, Jr., Fathers of the Church, vol. 37 [New York: Fathers of the
Church, 1958], pp. 352–54).

[58] Origen, *De Oratione* XXXI, 2.

After this general statement John Damascene proceeds to the "scriptural proof". Since the "light" and, accordingly, the "dawn" of the light in Sacred Scripture are metaphors for God and his Christ, the orient or the east is dedicated to the worship of God. The thought is familiar to us from Pseudo-Justin.[59]

What follows then is salvation history in the narrower sense, that is, first the *primordial story* of the Garden of Eden in the east and the settlement of Adam after his banishment "westward", "opposite Paradise".

Then, in the *Old Covenant*, the east recurs as the preferred point of the compass in various ways. John mentions the arrangement of the tent of the covenant, the order in which the tribes of Israel camped, and the temple of Solomon. From here, moreover, it is easy to extrapolate to the symbolism in the construction of Christian churches.

It is only consistent that the *New Covenant* as well—as the fulfillment and completion of the Old Covenant—should adopt the symbolic significance of "orientation". John Damascene mentions the crucifixion, ascension, and second coming of Christ; he had already alluded to his birth earlier in the passage: Christ is the "Orient" promised by the prophets; recall also the star "in the east" that the Magi saw and— remembering the prophetic promises of a "star out of Jacob"[60]—interpreted as a sign of the Messiah's birth.[61]

Thus the unwritten apostolic tradition of worshiping God while facing east has various reasons that complement one another and which John Damascene carefully notes in the course of the chapter. Since everything beautiful should be

[59] See above, pp. 57f.
[60] Num 24:17.
[61] Mt 2:1ff.

dedicated to God, the Author of all that is beautiful and good, and since the dawn is no doubt one of the most beautiful things, it should be reserved for the worship of God. This is a "cosmic" argument, then, that even a non-Christian could have formulated, which is why the east had a privileged place even in pre-Christian times and in non-biblical traditions, as we will see later. Nevertheless it is biblical man —the Christian, based on the fullness of revelation in which he shares, to a greater extent than the Jew—to whom *salvation history* discloses the entire theological depth of this "orientation". Facing the east, the Christian worships God with a view of the *"ancient fatherland"*, which he has been seeking since he was banished from Paradise. At the same time he thereby turns toward the *Crucified*, who through his death and Resurrection has opened again for us the gate to our original home, into which he has preceded us, as Luke 23:43 suggests. From thence, from the beginning, we await our Lord in his *second coming* in glory, which will bring the fulfillment of the promised salvation.

~

The weight and the depth of this theological interpretation of the orientation of prayer can scarcely fail to impress even modern man. Especially if he recognizes that this interpretation, besides what has been said on the subject, is also rooted in the symbolism of the *baptismal event*, to which he owes his status as a Christian. For this latter sacramental reason pertains immediately to his own existence. In the sacrament, what was bestowed upon humanity as a whole in salvation history is bestowed upon me in an utterly personal way.

> *When, therefore, you renounce Satan, utterly breaking all covenant with him, that ancient league with hell, there is opened to you the Paradise of God, which he planted toward the east, whence for*

his transgression our first father was exiled; and symbolic of this (σύμβολον) *was your turning from the west toward the east, the place of light.*[62]

The relation between the "east" and Christ is so close in the mind of the Fathers that Ambrose in the same context, with regard to the newly baptized turning from the west toward the east, can simply say: "Whoever renounces the devil turns toward Christ and looks at him directly."[63]

Whenever a Christian places himself in the presence of his Lord to pray, therefore—even if this is not always said explicitly or consciously adverted to—he *renews* with this turn toward the east that act of turning away from the evil one and of professing the triune God, which he performed once and for all in baptism.[64]

~

Considering what has been said thus far, it is no wonder that all other devotional practices have to yield to the "orientation" in prayer, no matter how meaningful and symbolic they may be in and of themselves. Therefore Origen, for example, writes:

Now there are still a few things to be said about the direction in which one should face while praying. Since there are four points of the compass, north and south, setting and rising [of the sun], who would not want to admit, without further discussion, that the direction facing sunrise clearly indicates that one must say one's

[62] Cyril of Jerusalem, *Catecheses Mystagogicae* I, 9 (English translation: R. W. Church, in F. L. Cross, ed., *St. Cyril of Jerusalem's Lectures on the Christian Sacraments* [London, 1966], pp. 57–58).

[63] Ambrose, *De Mysteriis* 7 (German ed.: J. Schmitz, Fontes Christiani 3 [Freiburg, 1990], pp. 208f.)

[64] As for the Sign of the Cross, which is pertinent in this connection, see below, pp. 179ff.

*prayers while symbolically bowing toward it, as though the soul
were looking to the "dawn of the true Light".*[65]

*However, if someone would rather bring his petition [before
God] at the opening of his door, no matter in what direction the
door of his house opens, reasoning that the view of the sky is much
more inviting than staring at the wall, if indeed the eastern side
of the house by chance has no opening, then this answer should
be given to him: Since the habitations of men open toward this
or that point of the compass by convention (θέσει), whereas the
east has precedence over the other points of the compass by nature
(φύσει), therefore what is natural is to be preferred over what is
conventional. But is it not true also that someone who wants to
pray outdoors will pray, according to this deliberation, facing east
rather than facing west? If the east is to be preferred there for a
reasonable cause, why should we not proceed in this way everywhere?*[66]

The man of antiquity, whether Jew or pagan, was in fact
accustomed to praying while facing the open sky, as we will
see later.[67] This cherished practice now had to yield, when
necessary, to the Christian "orientation", even at the risk of
finding oneself in front of a blank wall! Origen's statement
here is categorical: The choice of place and posture, and so
forth, in prayer may be adapted to circumstances from time
to time, but not the direction in which one prays. Turning
toward the orient excludes every other point of the compass.[68] "One must look [in that direction] under all circumstances"[69]—even when the reasons for the Church's tradition are not known to everyone.[70] Origen only hints here
at what these reasons are with his reference to the "dawn of

[65] Cf. Zech 6:12; Lk 1:78 (dawn); Jn 1:9 (true light).
[66] Origen, *De Oratione* XXXII.
[67] See below, pp. 157ff.
[68] Origen, *Num. hom.* V, 1 (Baehrens).
[69] Origen, *De Oratione* XXXI, 1.
[70] Origen, *Num. hom.* V, 1 (Baehrens).

the true Light"; they were, nonetheless, already essentially the same as the later Fathers mention.

~

The Fathers knew very well, moreover, that preferring the east over the other three points of the compass, and even orientation in prayer, is also attested outside the biblical revelation. The way in which they interpret this agreement is worth reconsidering in an age of worldwide encounters among the various religions.

> *Therefore the most ancient temples also faced toward the west, so that those who stood opposite the images of the gods were taught to turn toward the east.*[71]

That is to say, toward that "dawn" of the "eternal light",[72] from which the peoples arbitrarily moved away when they set out to build the Tower of Babel—a sacrilege, for which they were punished by God with the loss of the one language they had had in common until then.[73] Only Israel did not move away from this "orient" and therefore retained its "original language", the "language of the orient", which is also why, of all peoples, it alone became the "portion of the Lord",[74] as Origen deduces in a profound meditation.[75]

Without their becoming aware of it, then, the divine Pedagogue led the pagans, too, in the midst of their mistaken worship of idols, toward that "orient", namely, to their true "origin" (ἀρχή) whence "the light comes, which first shone out of the darkness",[76] that is to say, Christ, the "sun of

---

[71] Clement of Alexandria, *Stromata* VII, 43, 7.
[72] Wis 7:26.
[73] Cf. Gen 11:1ff.
[74] Deut 32:9.
[75] Origen, *Contra Celsum* V, 29ff. (Koetschau).
[76] Cf. 2 Cor 4:6.

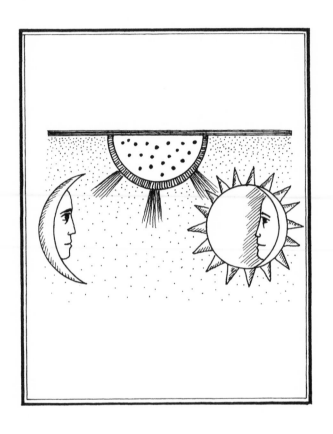

righteousness", who, for "those who wallow in ignorance,[77] makes the day of the knowledge of truth dawn after the manner of the sun."[78]

~

After all this, who would claim that "orientation" in prayer was an anachronistic side issue? When its meaning is understood and where it is consciously put into practice, it preserves the praying Christian from the flight into non-essentials—which today more than ever is a danger. The Muslim knows very well why he bows in prayer toward Mecca—with no regard whatsoever to the architecture of the room in which he happens to be. The Zen disciple, too, knows very well why he does not need such an "orientation" at all while meditating, since any thought of addressing "Another" is foreign to him.

And the Christian? He ought to know that his sanctification consists solely in union with God while completely maintaining his "otherness" as a person. After all, the "type", the pattern of this unconfused unity, which indeed makes it possible, is the unity of the three Divine Hypostases of God, who is essentially one (Evagrius). He is reminded of this precisely by turning his "face"—both spiritually and physically—to the east, toward the Lord!

3. "Seven times a day I praise Thee" (Ps 118:164)

On this earth, man is bound up with space and time. No less significant than the proper place, therefore, is the "suitable and chosen time" for prayer, as Origen remarked.

---

[77] Cf. Mt 4:16.
[78] Clement of Alexandria, *Stromata* VII, 43, 6.

We experience time as *ordered succession*, of sun and moon, of particular phases. Many of these successions repeat themselves cyclically; viewed as a whole, nevertheless, our lifetime runs in a straight line to its conclusion. One of the mysteries of the spiritual life, therefore, is *regularity*, which adapts to the rhythm of our life. It is the same as with any handicraft or art: it is not enough to play a few measures on the piano now and then in order to become a good pianist. "Practice makes perfect" is true of prayer as well. A "practicing Christian" is, to the mind of the holy Fathers, not a man who more or less faithfully fulfills his Sunday duty, but rather one who day after day, his whole life long, prays several times a day, that is, practices his faith *regularly*, just as he regularly performs other functions necessary for life —eating, sleeping, breathing . . . Only in this way will his "spiritual activity" attain that natural character that appears self-evident in the case of the functions just mentioned.

∼

For biblical man, both regular personal prayer and also participation in common prayer or the "cult" went without saying. Daniel bent the knee three times a day and prayed to God—facing Jerusalem, since he was, after all, in exile in Babylon.[79] This may well have been the universal custom of pious Jews. The psalms are full of allusions to such practices. The preferred times for prayer were obviously the *early morning*[80] and the *evening*[81] or else the *night*,[82] that is, the quietest times of the day. As we have seen, these are also

[79] Dan 6:10, 13.
[80] Ps 5:4; 58:17; 87:14; 91:3.
[81] Ps 54:18; 140:2.
[82] Ps 76:3, 7; 91:3; 118:55; 133:2.

the times at which Christ especially liked to withdraw for solitary prayer.

~

The practice of praying *three times a day*, namely, morning, noon, and evening,[83] or at the third, sixth, and ninth hours, is already a rule in the early Christian era.[84] The ancient Fathers trace it back to the apostles themselves, who in turn were probably only being faithful to the Jewish practice, as the example of Daniel teaches us. Thus Tertullian, for instance, writes between 200 and 206:

> *With regard to the times for prayer, nothing has been prescribed for us, except to pray "always"[85] and "in every place".[86]*

After discussing "in every place", which he intends to be understood as corresponding to decorum or necessity, so as not to contradict Matthew 6:5, he continues:

> *With regard to the times, though, the external observance of certain hours should not be something superfluous, namely, those common hours that mark off the major portions of the day, the third, sixth, and ninth hours, which one also finds in Scripture mentioned as the more excellent. The Holy Spirit was poured out upon the assembled disciples for the first time at the third hour.[87] On the day when Peter had the vision of the commonality [of Jews and Gentiles] in that container, he had gone up to the housetop at about the sixth hour to pray.[88] The same apostle went with*

---

[83] Ps 54:18.
[84] *Didache* 8, 3 (Rordorf/Tuilier).
[85] Lk 18:1.
[86] Tertullian, *De Oratione* 24; 1 Tim 2:8.
[87] Acts 2:15.
[88] Acts 10:9.

*John at the ninth hour to the temple, where he restored health to
the lame man.*[89]

Tertullian, then, does not see in this practice of the apostles a binding precept, but he still considers it good to give
prayer "a fixed form" through the observance of these times
of the day. "Aside from the obligatory prayers, naturally,
which we must say even without admonition at the beginning of the day and of the night", the Christian should therefore "pray to God no less often than at least three times a
day—since he is in debt to the three [Divine] Persons, the
Father, the Son, and the Holy Spirit".[90] Thus we would
have five daily prayer times, as they are still observed today
by the disciples of Muhammad.

"No less often than at least" clearly indicates that the
point of these fixed prayer times cannot be to limit prayer
to these times only, whether it be morning and evening or
five times a day or even "seven times a day",[91] as was later
the custom.

> *Even if some people set fixed hours for prayer, for instance, the
> third and the sixth and the ninth, against this it should be said that
> the Gnostic prays throughout his entire life, since he is striving to
> be united with God through prayer and, in a word, to have left
> everything behind that will be of no use to him there, as one who
> here below has already reached the perfection of manly maturity
> in love.*
>
> *But the division of the hours, too, with its three intervals that
> are marked with the same prayers, is familiar to those who know
> the blessed triad of the holy dwellings*[92] *[in heaven].*[93]

[89] Tertullian, *De Oratione* 25. Reference to Acts 3:1.
[90] Ibid.
[91] Ps 118:164.
[92] Cf. Clement of Alexandria, *Stromata* VI, 114, 3.
[93] Ibid., VII, 40, 3–4.

~

This ideal of the Christian "gnostic", that is, of the contemplative soul blessed with the true knowledge of God, an ideal that Clement of Alexandria formulated long before the development of organized monasticism, was later adopted by the disciples of Saint Anthony. The Desert Fathers knew of only two set *prayer times*, at the beginning and at the end of the night, and these were not even particularly long. During the remainder of the day and for a good part of the night they made use of a definite "method", as we will see later, in order to keep their "mind continually at prayer". Palestinian monasticism had a greater number of fixed prayer times. Thus, for example, Bishop Epiphanius of Salamis on the island of Cyprus, who was originally from Palestine, deduces seven prayer times from indications scattered throughout the Psalter.

> *[Epiphanius of Salamis] said: The prophet David prayed "before the watches of the night"*,[94] *arose "at midnight"*,[95] *cried out [to God] "before dawn"*,[96] *"in the morning"*[97] *he went into the presence of God, "at dawn" he begged, "[in the] evening and . . . at noon"*[98] *he petitioned, and therefore he said: "Seven times a day I praise thee."*[99]

Nevertheless, his ideal, too, was that of "continual prayer", which in essence is prescribed already in the psalms. After all, the psalmist assures us that he cried out to God "all day

[94] Ps 118:148.
[95] Ps 118:62.
[96] Ps 118:147.
[97] Ps 5:4.
[98] Ps 54:18.
[99] Epiphanius 7. Last citation is Ps 118:164.

long'',[100] or that he meditates on the Law "day and night'',[101] which is really to say *always*.

> *A message was sent to the blessed Epiphanius, the Bishop of [Salamis on] Cyprus, from the abbot of the monastery that he owned in Palestine: "Thanks to your prayers we have not neglected our Rule, but zealously observe not only the first but also the third, sixth, and ninth hour, as well as Vespers." He rebuked them, however, and sent the reply: "It is obvious that you neglect the other hours of the day if you cease from prayer. The true monk, indeed, must have prayer and psalmody in his heart "unceasingly"!*[102]

The observance of a fixed number of times of prayer, distributed throughout the day (and the night), which requires a certain self-discipline, has therefore essentially the sole purpose of building *bridges* that enable our inconstant mind to make its way across the river of time. Through this practice the mind acquires that *dexterity* and *facility of movement* which no artist or craftsman can do without. To be sure, this is in part simply routine, but it is necessary in order to accomplish what is really at stake: the *art*—of carpentry, of playing the violin, of playing soccer . . . —and, indeed, of praying, which is the highest and most perfect activity of our mind, as Evagrius assures us.[103] The better the training, the more perfectly natural the movement will seem to be, and the greater the joy, also, that we experience in the action.

∽

[100] Ps 31:3.
[101] Ps 1:2.
[102] 1 Thess 5:17; Epiphanius 3.
[103] Evagrius, *De Oratione* 84.

Nevertheless, as with every art, from time to time there are particular difficulties to overcome in the daily practice of prayer. The most formidable opponent is a certain *weariness*, often undefinable, which can set in even when there is no lack of necessary leisure time.

This state of repugnance, which was quite well known to the Fathers, too, can sometimes become so strong that the monk is no longer capable of reciting his daily office—at least he thinks so. If he gives in here, he ultimately reaches the point at which he doubts the meaning of his existence in the first place. This is wrong, because:

> *Battles like these occur as if through an abandonment on God's part, in order to put one's free will to the test and to determine where its inclination lies.*[104]

What should you do, then? You must force yourself, that is, activate the power of your will, so as to observe in any event the prescribed number of prayer times, even if the office itself has to be reduced to a minimum, one psalm, three Glory Bes, one Trisagion, and one genuflection—provided you are capable of it. If the soul's oppression is too great, one must make use of the ultimate remedy.

> *If this battle against you increases in force, my Brother, and stops your mouth and does not allow you to recite the office, not even in the way that I have described above, then force yourself to get on your feet and walk up and down in your cell, while saluting the Cross and making prostrations before it, and our Lord in his mercy will allow [this battle] to pass.*[105]

---

[104] Joseph Hazzaya (Joseph the Visionary), p. 140.
[105] Ibid., p. 144.

When words seem to have lost all meaning, the only thing remaining is the physical *gesture*, a theme to which we shall later return and treat in detail.

∿

4. *"Blessed is he who is awake!"* (Rev 16:15)

Modern man is accustomed to regard the night mainly as a time for well-earned rest. If he nevertheless stays awake voluntarily, then it is because his work requires it of him or because is celebrating a holiday, and so on. Biblical man and the Fathers slept, certainly, like every human being, yet for them the night was also the preferred time for prayer.

∿

How often it is mentioned in the psalms that the person who prays "meditates"[106] on the law of God not only by day, but also by night, that he stretches out his hands to God in prayer at night,[107] that he rises "at midnight to praise God because of his righteous ordinances"[108] . . . As we have already seen, even Christ was accustomed to spend "all night . . . in prayer to God",[109] or "in the morning, a great while before day" to go out into the wilderness to pray.[110]

Hence the Lord urgently admonishes his disciples, also, to "watch and pray"[111] and indicates a new reason for it: "You do not know the time" of the return of the Son of

[106] Ps 1:2
[107] Ps 76:3; 133:2.
[108] Ps 118:62.
[109] Lk 6:12.
[110] Mk 1:35.
[111] Mk 14:38; cf. Lk 21:36.

Man[112] and could therefore, weakened by sleep, "enter into temptation."[113]

We are urgently admonished by the Apostle as well, who according to his own testimony kept watch through many nights.[114] "Continue steadfastly in prayer, being watchful in it with thanksgiving."[115] These prayerful watches are not the least important thing that distinguishes the Christian from the drowsy children of this world.

> But you are not in darkness, brethren,
> for that day [of the Lord's second coming] to surprise you like
>   a thief.
> For you are all sons of light and sons of the day;
> we are not of the night or of darkness.
> So then let us not sleep, as others do,
> but let us keep awake and be sober.
> For those who sleep sleep at night,
> and those who get drunk are drunk at night.
> But, since we belong to the day,
> let us be sober.[116]

~

The early Church immediately took to heart the example of Christ and of the apostles and put their teachings into practice. Watching and waking belongs to the oldest customs of the primitive Church.

---

[112] Mk 13:33 and parallel passages.
[113] Cf. Mt 26:41 and parallel passages.
[114] 2 Cor 6:5; 11:27.
[115] Col 4:2; cf. Eph 6:18.
[116] 1 Thess 5:4ff.

Watch over your lives. Your lamps should not go out[117] *nor your loins be ungirded;*[118] *be ready instead. For you do not know the hour when our Lord is coming.*[119]

The true Christian is like a soldier. Prayer is his "fortified wall of faith" and his "weapon of defense and attack against the enemy who lies in ambush for us on every side." Therefore he "never proceeds unarmed".

Let us not forget to stand at our post by day, nor to watch at night! Equipped with the weapon of prayer, we will guard the standard of our commander-in-chief and, praying, wait for the angel's trumpet.[120]

This "eschatological note" of waiting for the return of the Lord was handed down by the first Christians, who still had to prove their faith, often in the midst of bloody persecutions, and carried on by those "soldiers of Christ", as the early monks regarded themselves.

One can see them, indeed, [living] scattered in the wilderness, [where they] like true sons await their Father, Christ, or as an army watches for its king, or an honorable household servant awaits his master and liberator. Among them there is no thought of clothing or concern for food, but only in [the singing of] hymns,[121] *of looking forward to the coming of Christ.*[122]

They also arranged the entire course of their day with respect to this goal.

[117] Cf. Mt 25:8.
[118] Lk 12:35.
[119] *Didache* 16:1. The last reference is to Mt 24:42, 44.
[120] Tertullian, *De Oratione* 29.
[121] Cf. Eph 5:19.
[122] *Historia Monachorum in Aegypto*, Prol. 7 (Festugière).

As for sleep at night, pray for two hours beginning at evening,
reckoning them from sunset on.[123] *And after you have praised*
[God], sleep for six hours.[124] *Then arise for the night watch and*
spend the remaining four hours [until sunrise] in prayer.[125] *In the*
summer, do the same; with the hours curtailed and fewer psalms,
though, because of the shortness of the nights.[126]

Since precision clocks were not yet available, time was
measured by the number of psalm verses that convention-
ally could be recited in an hour.[127] Six hours of sleep, half
the night,[128] is a quite reasonable amount. Only the *rising*
at night demands a certain degree of willpower. No wonder,
then, that as time went on the original zeal was in danger
of growing weak, even among clerics. Therefore the great
ascetic Nilus of Ancyra sternly admonishes the deacon Jor-
danes:

If Christ, the Lord of all, "continued in prayer all night"[129]
because he wanted to teach us to watch and to pray, and also
"about midnight Paul and Silas were praying and singing hymns
to God,"[130] *and the prophet says: "At midnight I rise to praise*
thee, because of thy righteous ordinances,"[131]—*I marvel at how*
you, who sleep and snore all night, are not condemned by your
conscience! Therefore may you also resolve to shake off death-

[123] That is, approximately from 6:00 P.M. to 8:00 P.M.

[124] From 8:00 P.M. to 2:00 A.M.

[125] From 2:00 A.M. to 6:00 A.M.

[126] Barsanuphios and John, *Epistula* 146.

[127] Ibid., *Epistula* 147.

[128] Ibid., *Epistula* 158. In the monastic desert it was customary to
sleep for one-third of the night, i.e., about four hours. Cf. Evagrius,
Vita D (with note).

[129] Lk 6:12.

[130] Acts 16:25.

[131] Ps 118:62.

dealing sleep and to dedicate yourself untiringly to prayer and psalmody.[132]

~

Watching and praying, which evidently was not always easy for the Fathers, either, and which always requires a certain amount of willpower, was therefore never merely an ascetical test of strength aimed at "conquering nature". "Nature" mistreated in such a way would sooner or later settle accounts on its own.

Biblical man and the Fathers held watching and praying in high esteem for various reasons. The eschatological "waiting for the Lord", which really ought to characterize every Christian, has already been mentioned. It imparts an entirely new quality to *time*, in that it sets a fixed goal for its endless streaming and thus impresses its own stamp on the whole of life, which strives toward this goal. "Living for today" is something quite different from realizing the uncertainty of the "day of the Lord" and therefore wisely "making the most of the time".[133]

Watching and waking brings about in the praying Christian that "sobriety" which guards him against being overcome with sleep and against the intoxication of the children of darkness. In turn, sobriety of the mind, which (in contrast to the "coarsening" effect of sleep) "refines" the mind, makes the one who keeps watch receptive to the contemplation of the divine mysteries.

Sleep flees from the one who, like Jacob, watches his flocks at night,[134] *and if it still takes hold of him, then this sleep is for*

[132] Nilus of Ancyra, *Epistula* III, 127 (PG 79, 444 A).
[133] Eph 5:15f.
[134] Cf. Gen 31:40.

him like waking is for someone else. The fire with which his heart
burns simply does not allow him to be submerged in sleep. Indeed,
he sings psalms with David: "Lighten my eyes, lest I sleep the
sleep of death."[135]

The one who has arrived at this degree and has tasted its sweet-
ness understands what has been said. For such a one has not be-
come drunk with material sleep, but only makes use of natural
sleep.[136]

What this "degree" and its "sweetness" mean is suggested
by a saying of Anthony, the father of monasticism, which
was handed down to us by John Cassian, who heard it himself from Abba Isaac.

So that you may grasp, however, what the condition of true prayer
is, I will present to you, not my teaching, but that of blessed An-
thony. From him we know that he sometimes continued so long
in prayer that we often heard him cry out in an ardent spirit,
when he prayed in ecstasy and the light of the rising sun began
to pour forth: "Why do you hinder me, O sun, since you only
rise this early so as to draw me away from that clarity of the true
Light?"[137]

Indeed, Evagrius assures us that our mind can see the intelligible, spiritual world only with difficulty during the day-
time, because our senses are drawn away by the things that
are clearly visible in the sunlight and thus distract the mind.
At night, though, it can see the spiritual world *during prayer*
time, when it reveals itself to him, completely surrounded
by light . . .[138] To Evagrius himself was granted such a rev-

---

[135] Ps 12:4.
[136] Barsanuphios and John, *Epistula* 321.
[137] Cassian, *Conlationes* IX, 31 (Petschenig).
[138] Evagrius, *Kephalaia Gnostika* V, 42 (Guillaumont).

elation of the spiritual world, as he watched at night and meditated on the book of one of the prophets.[139]

~

Nowadays those who belong to a strict, so-called "contemplative" order are practically the only ones who still "watch and pray", that is, arise in the middle of the night and pray the Divine Office as a community. The hectic pace of modern life, which is forever ruled by the clock indicating the minutes and the seconds, is not very conducive to this practice. People in antiquity lived a more tranquil life. The day between sunrise (about 6:00 A.M.) and sunset (about 6:00 P.M.) was subdivided into intervals of three hours each; hence the traditional prayer times at the third, sixth and ninth hour, that is, at 9:00 A.M., 12:00 noon, and 3:00 P.M.

"Lately, in these times" even the majority of monks have to be content with less than that. Christ's example and the rule stated in the letter of the recluse John of Gaza (cited above) make clear, nevertheless, what is at stake and how one can still "watch and pray" even today. For even Christ would hardly have spent *every* night in prayer. Evidently, though, he was accustomed to withdraw to pray alone in the late evening, after sunset, or else "in the early morning, a great while before daylight", as any devout soul who prayed the psalms would do. These are precisely the times that the Fathers, too, generally reserved for prayer. The individual will have to determine the quantity on the basis of his own experience, together with the advice of his spiritual father, who will take into account age, health, and spiritual maturity. One thing is certain, in any case: Without the

[139] Evagrius, *Vita* J.

effort of watching and waking, no one attains that spiritual "sobriety" that the monk Hesychios from Mount Sinai so extravagantly praises.

> *How lovely and delightful, luminous and pleasing, extraordinary, radiant, and beautiful a virtue is sobriety, when with thee, Christ our God, and accompanied by the great humility of the watchful human intellect!*
>
> *For indeed, it sends out "to the sea and its depths" its branches of contemplation, and "to the river its shoots"*[140] *of delightful, divine mysteries. Sobriety is like Jacob's ladder, upon which God rests and the angels ascend.*[141]

$\sim$

5. *"With prayer and fasting"* (Acts 14:23)

Since biblical times another bodily exercise has been just as closely connected with prayer as watching and waking: fasting, which should not go unmentioned, still less because it has been associated, since time immemorial, with designated *seasons*. For most people in the Western world today it is known, if at all, only in the secularized form of "dieting". The "Great Lenten Fast" before Easter, for instance, makes no difference to the daily life even of practicing Christians. That was not always the case, as we have said, and it is still quite otherwise in the Christian East.

$\sim$

[140] Cf. Ps 79:12.
[141] Hesychios to Theodulos, c. 50/51 (*Philokalia*, 1:149 [Athens, 1957]).

Since time immemorial prayer and fasting have been so intimately connected that they are already mentioned together in many passages of Sacred Scripture, for "prayer is good when accompanied by fasting."[142] The aged prophetess Anna worshiped "with prayer and fasting night and day",[143] as did Paul[144] and the early Christian community.[145] This custom is so firmly anchored in the early Christian tradition that many copyists spontaneously add the word "fasting" to "prayer", even where it—probably—did not stand originally, for instance, Matthew 17:21; Mark 9:29; 1 Corinthians 7:5.

At first glance it might appear that the early Christian practice of fasting could not be based on Christ's word and example and, indeed, would directly contradict them. Of course Christ once fasted forty days and forty nights in the desert,[146] but otherwise he seemed to many people to be rather a "glutton and a drunkard",[147] because he did not hesitate to eat with "tax collectors and sinners" and sometimes even took the initiative himself to do so. Consequently he was open to the question, why the disciples of John and the disciples of the Pharisees "fast often and offer prayers", while his disciples did not.[148] Did Paul and the early Christian community in fact misunderstand Christ when they ended up imitating the disciples of John and those of the Pharisees?

[142] Tob 12:8.
[143] Lk 2:37.
[144] 2 Cor 6:5; cf. 11:27.
[145] Acts 13:3.
[146] Mt 4:2 and parallel passages.
[147] Mt 11:19.
[148] Lk 5:33.

By no means, for Christ did not reject fasting any more than he rejected prayer. In both cases, nevertheless, he was concerned with guarding his disciples against every sort of *hypocrisy* and vain display of their own "piety".

> *And when you fast, do not look dismal, like the hypocrites, for they disfigure their faces that their fasting may be seen by men. Truly, I say to you, they have their reward.*
>
> *But when you fast, anoint your head and wash your face, that your fasting may not be seen by men but by your Father who is in secret; and your Father who sees in secret will reward you.*[149]

It is with fasting just as it is with prayer: The disciples of Jesus also fast, naturally, but they do it solely *for God's sake*, not in order to be seen and praised. The same goes for almsgiving and ultimately for the practice of all the virtues. The Fathers, who were noted for the severity of their fasts, took that very much to heart. It is especially true of fasting that one should "seal up the good odor of one's [ascetical] efforts with silence".

> *Just as you conceal your sins from men, conceal from them also your efforts!*[150]

In all this it was far from the intentions of the Fathers to overestimate the value of the corporal "works" and hence of fasting.

> *Someone asked an elder, "How do I find God?" And he said, "By fasting, by watching, by labors, by mercy, and, above all these, by discernment. For I say to you, many have tormented their flesh without discernment and have gone away empty, without getting anything for it. Our mouth has an evil smell from*

---

[149] Mt 6:16–18.
[150] Evagrius, *Ad Eulogium* 14 (PG 79, 1112 B).

fasting, we know the Scriptures by heart, we have recited all of David [that is, the Psalter]—and yet what God is seeking we do not have: love and humility."[151]

~

Christ had, nevertheless, a very concrete reason for disregarding the customary fasts that were generally observed at that time among the "holy ones of Israel" and for exempting his disciples from them: *the presence of the "Bridegroom".*[152] In this brief, privileged time of his presence, there is another concern: "The kingdom of God is at hand; repent, and believe in the gospel!"[153] Christ made use of the common meal as a preferred method of bringing to all the good news of reconciliation and the call to conversion: the chiefs of the Pharisees,[154] influential tax collectors[155] as well as "sinners" of every sort.[156] A common meal as a sign of reconciliation —another teaching that the Desert Fathers took very seriously to heart.

> *When your brother grieves you,*
> *bring him into your house*
> *and do not hesitate to enter into his,*
> *but rather eat your food with him.*
> *By doing this, indeed,*
> *you will save your soul,*
> *and during the time of prayer*
> *you will encounter no difficulty.*[157]

[151] Nau 222.
[152] Mt 9:15.
[153] Mk 1:15.
[154] Lk 7:36ff.
[155] Lk 19:1ff.
[156] Mt 9:10f. etc.
[157] Evagrius, *Ad Monachos* 15 (Gressmann).

For it is generally the case that "a gift in secret averts anger", as Solomon the wise once said.[158] The Desert Fathers had scarcely any possessions they could have given as gifts. Therefore, "we, who are poor, will make up for our neediness by means of the table", is Evagrius' advice.[159] "Fasting , therefore, is indeed a useful thing, but it depends on our free choice."[160]

It is different with the divine commandment of love: it renders void all other human practices, however useful they may be. For the commandment of hospitality rescinded the rules about fasting, too, even when one then had to prepare a table six times a day . . .[161]

> Once two brothers came to a certain elder. The elder, though, had the custom of eating only on certain days. Now when he saw the brothers, he rejoiced and said: "Fasting has its reward. On the other hand, he who eats out of charity fulfills two commandments, for he renounces his own will and fulfills the commandment [of love]." And he gave the brothers refreshment.[162]

Always keeping this commandment of love in mind, Christ's disciples were in no way inferior to the disciples of the Pharisees and those of John the Baptist, with regard to fasting, after "the Bridegroom was taken away from them,"[163] even if it was their hallowed practice to fast, not on Monday and Thursday as the Jews did, but rather on Wednesday and Friday.[164]

[158] Prov 21:14.
[159] Evagrius, *Praktikos* 26.
[160] Cassian 1.
[161] Cassian 3.
[162] Nau 288.
[163] Mt 9:15.
[164] *Didache* 8, 1 (Rordorf/Tuilier).

Since fasting, nevertheless, is one of the *penitential practices*, it goes without saying that from the very beginning exceptions were made for those days on which Christians call to mind the return of Christ the "Bridegroom".

> *From Saturday evening, the vigil of the Lord's day, until the following evening, one does not bend the knee among the Egyptians, and it is the same during the entire time of Pentecost [between Easter and Pentecost], and in this season the rule of fasting is not observed, either.*[165]

~

If fasting, then, like all bodily "austerities" of this sort, has only relative value, what is its purpose? The psalmist himself mentions an initial reason for fasting: It humbles the soul,[166] in contrast to feasting, which lifts up the heart until it falls away from God.[167] For disciplining the body by fasting reminds man in a perceptible way that "Man shall not live by bread alone, but by every word that proceeds from the mouth of God", to whom, furthermore, he is indebted for the life-sustaining bread as well. It was precisely for the sake of this experience that God "humbled" the people of Israel in the desert and "let them hunger".[168]

Hence the spiritual meaning of fasting is, first of all, to make the soul humble. "Indeed, nothing humbles the soul as does fasting,"[169] since it causes the soul to experience in a fundamental way its complete *dependence upon God.*

---

[165] Cassian, *De Institutis* II, 18 (Petschenig).

[166] Ps 34:13.

[167] Cf. Deut 8:12ff.; 32:15, etc.

[168] Deut 8:3.

[169] Evagrius, *In Ps. 34:13* ξ.

The obstacles to this humility of heart are our manifold "passions", those "sicknesses of the soul" that do not allow it to behave "naturally", that is, according to the purpose for which it was created. Now fasting is an excellent means of "covering over" these passions, as Evagrius says in an allegorical interpretation of a psalm verse.

Fasting is a covering for the soul, which conceals its passions, that is, shameful desires and irrational anger. Therefore he who does not fast exposes himself indecently,[170]

like Noah when he was drunk,[171] to whom Evagrius is alluding here. This means that the purpose of bodily fasting is to cleanse the soul of its shameful vices and to instill a humble attitude. Without this "purity of heart", even the thought of "true prayer" would be sacrilege.

Whoever is [still] caught up in sins and outbursts of anger and dares to reach out shamelessly after the knowledge of divine things or even to enter [the place] of immaterial prayer, let him expect to hear the Apostle's reproach, according to which it is not safe for him "to pray with head uncovered". Indeed, such a soul, he says, "should have an 'authority' on her head, because of the angels,"[172] *by wrapping herself fittingly in shame and humility.*[173]

∼

Besides this, fasting has a very practical significance, too:

A famished stomach
    enables one to watch in prayer,

---

[170] Ibid., 68, 11 v.
[171] Gen 9:21.
[172] 1 Cor 11:5, 11.
[173] Evagrius, *De Oratione* 145.

> *whereas a full stomach*
>   *brings about plentiful sleep.*[174]

And this practical usefulness has, in turn, a spiritual purpose, which is ultimately the sole concern.

> *A dirty mirror*
>   *does not reflect clearly the figure that falls upon it,*
> *and thinking that has been dulled by satiety*
>   *does not receive the knowledge of God.*[175]
> *The prayer of the one who fasts*
>   *is a high-flying young eagle,*
> *but that of the glutton who is burdened by satiety*
>   *is brought down.*[176]
> *The intellect of the one who fasts*
>   *is a shining star in a clear sky,*
> *but that of the glutton*
>   *remains shrouded in a moonless night.*[177]

In other words, just like watching and waking, fasting also prepares the mind of the one who prays for the contemplation of the divine mysteries.

Although fasting is therefore just as indispensable as watching to anyone who wants to "pray in truth", still, like everything in the spiritual life, it must take place "at the appropriate times and in moderation". In this respect each person will have his own suitable measure, according to his strength, his age, the circumstances of his life, and so on.

---

[174] Evagrius, *De Octo Spiritibus Malitiae*, I, 12 (PG 79, 1145 B).
[175] Ibid., I, 17.
[176] Ibid., I, 14.
[177] Ibid., I, 15.

For what is immoderate and untimely is of short duration. Something that lasts only a short time, though, is more likely harmful than useful.[178]

[178] Evagrius, *Praktikos* 15.

Chapter III

Manners of Praying

Among those things Origen considers necessary in order to describe prayer exhaustively, he mentions in the first place the "disposition" (κατάστασις) in the soul of the person praying. As an example of this essential inner disposition, he cites the words of Paul that the Christian should pray "without anger or disputes".[1] This freedom from anger or "thoughts" (διαλογισμῶν)[2] is a fruit of the "practical manner" of prayer (Evagrius) as a means of purification from the passions—above all from anger—since they are the worst opponents of "pure prayer", and from "thoughts" about them, and finally from all "mental images".

As Origen goes on to say in the same context, this "disposition" of the soul is always reflected in the body's posture as well; in the next chapter we will return to this subject and discuss it in detail. But the disposition is also reflected in the *manner* in which we pray. These ways and the spiritual dispositions that are expressed in them will be the topic of this chapter.

∼

---

[1] 1 Tim 2:8.

[2] The Fathers understood such "disputes" to include (wicked) "thoughts" as well. Cf. Evagrius, *Mal. cog.* 32 (Géhin-Guillaumont).

1. *"Prayers and supplications with loud cries and tears"*
   (Heb 5:7)

No one is surprised when someone sheds tears because he is grief-stricken. Tears of joy are probably familiar to most people as well. But tears in prayer? For the Fathers, in fact, tears and prayer belonged together inseparably and were by no means considered a sign of inappropriate sentimentality. This is true for the men of the Bible as well.

> *Hear my prayer, O LORD,*
> *and give ear to my cry;*
> *hold not thy peace at my tears!*[3]

Thus tears principally accompany "supplication" (δέησις). In tears a distraught father asks that his son be cured,[4] and in tears the sinful woman wordlessly asks Christ for forgiveness.[5] Even Christ, "in the days of his flesh . . . offered up prayers and supplications, with loud cries and tears, to him who was able to save him from death."[6]

~

Tears belong to the "practical manner" of prayer, for they are part of the labors of *praktike*, that is, the first stage of the spiritual life.

[3] Ps 38:13.
[4] Mk 9:24.
[5] Lk 7:38.
[6] Heb 5:7.

"Those who sow in tears, will reap with shouts of joy:"
  Those who complete praktike *amidst toil and tears "sow in tears". In contrast, those who effortlessly receive the knowledge [of God] "reap with shouts of joy".*[7]

Why this insistence on the necessity of tears, which appears so strange to modern men? Is the Christian not supposed to be joyful instead? Certainly, but the Fathers viewed the human condition more realistically perhaps than we do.

Abba Longinos had great contrition when he prayed and recited the psalms. One day his disciple asked him, "Abba, is this a spiritual rule, that a monk should weep all the time he is praying his office?" And the elder answered, "Yes, my child, this is the rule that God now demands of us. For in the beginning God did not create man so that he might weep, but rather so that he might rejoice and be glad and might glorify him, as pure and sinless as the angels. Once he fell into sin, however, he needed tears. And all who have fallen need them just the same. For where there are no sins, no tears will be necessary."[8]

~

At this first stage of the spiritual life, then, the principal concern is with what the Scripture and the Fathers call "repentance", "conversion", and "a change of heart" (μετάνοια). The very thought of such a conversion, however, is met with unexpected interior resistance. Evagrius speaks in this

---

[7] Evagrius, *In Ps.* 125:5 γ. Evagrius repeats this empirical fact rather often, cf. *In Ps.* 29:6 ε; 134:7 ε; *Praktikos* 90.
  [8] Nau 561.

regard about a certain interior "wildness" (ἀγριότης) or spiritual "insensitivity" (ἀναισθησία)[9] and dullness, which is overcome only with the help of tears of spiritual "sorrow" (πένθος).

> *Pray first for the gift of tears, so as to soften through contrition the wildness that dwells in your soul, so that by "confessing your transgressions to the LORD",*[10] *you may obtain forgiveness from him.*[11]

Every man is probably acquainted with this "wildness" in the form of that oppressive state of soul that the Fathers call *acedia, taedium cordis* (John Cassian), weariness of soul, boredom, empty indifference . . . Against this, tears are a powerful antidote.

> *Oppressive is sadness,*
> *   and boredom—insupportable,*
> *But tears offered to God*
> *   are mightier than both.*[12]

It is also true, conversely, that "the spirit of acedia drives tears away, and the spirit of sadness chafes at prayer."[13] What is to be done, then, when one is caught in the predicament of interior dryness and sadness? Evagrius recommends that one should then

---

[9] *Mal. cog.* 11 (Géhin-Guillaumont; PG 79, 1212 D).
[10] Cf. Ps 31:5.
[11] Evagrius, *De Oratione* 5.
[12] Evagrius, *Ad Virginem* 39 (Gressmann).
[13] Evagrius, *Ad Monachos* 56 (Gressmann).

divide the soul tearfully into two halves, one of which comforts
while the other is comforted, and to do this by sowing for ourselves
a good hope and by singing to ourselves the enchanting words of
David:

"Why art thou sad, O my soul? and why dost thou trouble
me? Hope in God; for I will still give praise to him: the salvation
of my countenance and my God."[14]

~

However pleasing to the Lord a prayer offered tearfully may
be,[15] tears must not become an *end in themselves*! Indeed, inherent in every human ascetical practice, insofar as it is man's
doing, is the fatal tendency to make itself autonomous. The
means suddenly becomes the end.

Even if you shed streams of tears as you pray, do not therefore
become at all presumptuous in your heart, as though you stood
high above the crowd. For your prayer has simply received [di-
vine] assistance, which enables you to confess your sins eagerly
and makes the Lord favorably inclined toward you through these
tears.

Therefore do not turn the defense against the passions into a
passion itself, lest you anger the Giver of the grace even more![16]

Someone who loses sight of the purpose of tears, that
is, the "extremely bitter conversion",[17] is in danger of "los-

---

[14] Evagrius, *Praktikos* 27. Quoting Ps 41:6, 12; 42:5 (LXX).
[15] Evagrius, *De Oratione* 6.
[16] Ibid., 7.
[17] Evagrius, *In Ps.* 79:6 γ.

ing his reason and going astray".[18] Conversely, it is also true that no one should imagine that he as a "proficient" soul no longer has need of tears.

If it seems to you that you no longer need tears on account of sins as you pray, then take heed of how far you have strayed from God, whereas you ought to be with him constantly, and then you will shed tears even more bitterly.[19]

This warning stems from a sober appreciation of human reality, and it is true, moreover, for the *"praktike"* in its entirety. Thus Evagrius, for instance, warns his "gnostic", the contemplative man, as "one who has been deemed worthy of knowledge":

Saint Paul "chastised his body and brought it into subjection."[20] *As long as you live, then, do not neglect your way of life or subject freedom from passions* (apatheia) *to reproach, abasing it by fattening your body.*[21]

Even when a man has attained the goal of the "practical life", the state of interior peace of soul, tears do not just vanish! At this stage, however, they are the expression of *humility* and as such are a guarantee that this state of peace is genuine (as opposed to the many forms of demonic counterfeits).[22] Therefore the Fathers consider tears to be in fact a sign of *a man's nearness to God*, as Evagrius has already suggested.

---

[18] Evagrius, *De Oratione* 8.
[19] Ibid., 78.
[20] 1 Cor 9:27.
[21] Evagrius, *Gnostikos* 37 (Guillaumont).
[22] Evagrius, *Praktikos* 57.

An elder once said: "A man who sits in his cell and meditates on the psalms is like a man who stands outside [the palace] and asks to see the king. The one who "prays constantly" is like the one who speaks with the king. The one who begs tearfully, though, is like the one who embraces the king's feet and asks for his mercy, like that prostitute who by her tears washed all her sins away in a short time."[23]

To be sure, God did not create man to weep, but rather to rejoice, as one of the Fathers used to say. Still, in Adam all have fallen and therefore all have need of tears, just as all need repentance and conversion. To recognize this is a sign of honest humility. Later we will hear this said about the so-called "prostrations", which in a gesture express the same thing that tears do.

"The nearer a man is to God, the more he feels that he is a sinner", one of the Fathers has said, because only God's holiness makes our sinfulness truly visible. Hence tears are not only found at the beginning of the spiritual path of conversion, but also accompany the penitent as far as his goal, where they are then transformed into "spiritual tears and a certain joy of heart", which the Fathers esteemed as a sign of the immediate action of the Holy Spirit and thus of nearness to God.[24]

∼

---

[23] Nau 572. Referring to Lk 7:38, 47.
[24] Diadochos of Photike, c. LXXIII; see below, pp. 135f.

2. *"Pray constantly"* (I Thess 5:17)

A "prayer", as commonly imagined, is a text—whether freely improvised or ready-made in a set form—something along the lines of the Our Father, the preeminent prayer of Christians. Such a "prayer", therefore, has a predetermined length and sometimes, like the Our Father, is even relatively short.

"To pray", then, means either turning to God and speaking freely or else making use of a text composed for this purpose. However long one may pray in this way, though, his "conversation with God" is necessarily limited in time.

Jesus' command to "pray at all times"[25] and Paul's exhortation, "pray constantly"[26] would then mean nothing more than to pray *frequently*, indeed very frequently. The early monastic Fathers, though, in contrast to some Fathers of the Church, nevertheless understood these commands in an absolutely literal sense.

> *It has not been prescribed for us to work, to watch, and to fast constantly, yet it has been commanded that we "pray constantly". This is because the first-mentioned activities, which heal the passionate part of the soul, require for their exercise the body also, which owing to its characteristic weakness would not be equal to these efforts. Prayer, on the other hand, makes the intellect strong and pure for the battle, since the intellect usually prays even without this body and fights against the demons on behalf of all the powers of the soul.[27]*

That the command of Paul is to be taken literally was a foregone conclusion not only for Evagrius; the early monastic Fathers were of the same opinion. Though the principle

[25] Lk 18:1.
[26] I Thess 5:17.
[27] Evagrius, *Praktikos* 49.

was well established, its realization in practice still raised questions.

> Question: *How can anyone "pray at all times"? For the body becomes tired during the liturgy.*
>
> Answer: *"Prayer" means not only standing during the time of prayer, but also [praying] "at all times".*
>
> Question: *How [is] "at all times" [to be understood]?*
>
> Answer: *Whether you eat, drink, or walk along the road or do some work or other, do not refrain from prayer.*
>
> Question: *Now if one is conversing with somebody, how can one fulfill the [command] "pray at all times"?*
>
> Answer: *In this regard the Apostle said: "[Pray at all times in the Spirit,] with all prayer and supplication."*[28] *While you are conversing with someone else, then, if you do not apply yourself to prayer, "pray with a supplication".*
>
> Question: *What prayer should be prayed?*
>
> Answer: *The "Our Father, who art in heaven", and so on.*
>
> Question: *What is the proper quantity of prayer?*
>
> Answer: *No quantity was set [for us]. For "at all times" and "pray without ceasing" are not quantifiable. Indeed, a monk who prays only when he sets out to pray does not really pray at all.*
>
> Then he added: *"Anyone who wants to accomplish this must regard all people as one man"*[29] *and refrain from wicked gossip.*[30]

"At all times" and "praying constantly" therefore means nothing less than praying *always and everywhere*, and that not as something done besides other activities, but rather at the same time with them! How this is to be accomplished we do not learn here, yet a precise reading of the Father's answer re-

[28] Eph 6:18.

[29] Evagrius, *De Oratione* 125: "A monk is someone who considers himself to be one with all, because it always appears to him that he is seeing himself in every person." That means, "Loving your neighbor as yourself."

[30] J.-G. Guy, "Un entretien monastique sur la contemplation", *Recherches de Sciences Religieuses* 50 (1962): 230ff. (nr. 18–22).

veals an important distinction between "prayer" (προσευχή) and "supplication" (δέησις). As an example of the first he mentions the Our Father, which usually was recited aloud; what form the latter would take, we do not learn here. The reference to Ephesians 6:18 only hints that it occurs somehow "in the spirit".

Hence we will inquire first about the "technique" of "unceasing prayer" and about the "method" for learning and practicing it.

~

Through the *The Way of a Pilgrim*[31] and the *Philokalia*,[32] that book of the holy Fathers that the pilgrim carried with him constantly, many have become acquainted with those specifically hesychastic methods that the Byzantine monks developed in the thirteenth and fourteenth centuries, that is, sitting on a low stool, with a bent-over posture, controlling the breathing, and so on. These methods, which are meant for "hesychasts", that is, for monks who live in absolute seclusion, may be practiced only under the direction of an experienced teacher and thus are always accessible to only a few. In contrast, what we know of the practices of the early Fathers is, in its simplicity, attainable by a greater number.[33]

[31] *The Way of a Pilgrim* and *The Pilgrim Continues His Way*, trans. R. M. French (London, 1930; New York: Seabury Press, 1965); see also the new translation in Classics of Western Spirituality, *The Pilgrim's Tale* (Mahwah, N.J., 2000).

[32] See *Writings from the Philokalia on Prayer of the Heart*, trans. E. Kadloubovsky and G. E. H. Palmer (London and Boston: Faber and Faber, 1951); The *Philokalia: The Complete Text*, comp. St. Nikodimos of the Holy Mountain and St. Makarios of Corinth, trans. G. E. H. Palmer, Philip Sherrard, and Kallistos Ware, 4 vols. (London; Boston: Faber and Faber, 1979–1995).

[33] For what follows, cf. G. Bunge, *Das Geistgebet*, (Cologne, 1987), pp. 29ff. ("Betet ohne Unterlass").

The Egyptian Desert Fathers very early on had their own traditions and customs. To be sure, these reflect to some extent their particular way of life, but it still can be said that they arranged their whole way of life according to the goal for which they strove.

> The hours and odes [of the Divine Office] are ecclesiastical traditions, and they are good in that they bring about a unison of the entire people; the same is true for the [cloistered] communities that are for the sake of unison among many. The monks of Scetis, however, neither have set hours nor recite odes, but [living alone, they occupy themselves with] manual labor, meditation, and prayers at short intervals. As for Vespers, the monks of Scetis recite twelve psalms, and at the end of each psalm, instead of the doxology, they say "Alleluia" and pray a prayer. They do the same at Night [Prayer of the Divine Office]: twelve psalms, and after the psalms they sit down to do their handwork.[34]

The monks of the desert of Scetis knew of only two "hours" of the Divine Office: *Vespers* after sunset and the *Vigil*, a four-hour night watch until sunrise,[35] which consisted in part of manual labor as well, to which they devoted practically the entire day besides. The Pachomian monks did not set this handwork aside even during common prayer, since it does not distract the mind but, on the contrary, helps to recollect it. Those who lived in the Scetis, for instance that monk to whom John of Gaza writes, customarily did as follows:

> When you sit down to your handwork, you should learn by heart or recite psalms. At the end of each psalm you should pray sitting: "O God, have mercy on me, a miserable man."[36] When you are

---

[34] Barsanuphios and John, *Epistula* 143.
[35] Ibid., 146, cited above on pp. 80f.
[36] Cf. Ps 50:3.

troubled by thoughts, then add: "O God, you see my affliction, come to my aid."[37]

Once you have made three rows of the net, then stand up to pray, and when you have bent the knee and likewise when you stand up again, pray the prayer just mentioned.[38]

The "method", then, is simple enough to be feasible. It consists of interrupting one's *work*, in this case making nets, at determined "short intervals", so as to rise for prayer and the prostration that goes along with it. In this way Makarios of Alexandria and his pupil Evagrius, for instance, offered up one hundred prayers a day[39] and, accordingly, one hundred genuflections. This seems to have been the usual "rule";[40] nevertheless other figures are given, since each one had his individual "measure".[41]

During the work the mind was not idle, either, but occupied itself with "meditation", that is, the contemplative repetition of Scripture verses, very often psalms, which were *learned by heart* for precisely this purpose. Each "meditation" of this sort was followed by very short *ejaculatory prayers*, that could be prayed sitting. Their content was not fixed and, once a particular "formula" was adopted, it could be modified at will. Neither the "prayers" mentioned above nor these ejaculations were particularly long, and they did not need to be, either.

As for the duration of the prayer, when you stand [for prayer] or "pray unceasingly", as the Apostle says, then you do not need

[37] Cf. Ps 69:6.

[38] Barsanuphios and John, *Epistula* 143.

[39] Palladios, *Historia Lausiaca* 20 (Butler, pp. 63, 13ff.) and 38 (Butler, p. 120, 11).

[40] J 741 (Regnault, *Série des anonymes*, p. 317).

[41] Cf. L. Regnault, "La prière continuelle 'monologistos'. . .", *Irénikon* 48 (1975): pp. 479ff.

*to prolong [the prayer] when you stand up. For throughout the
entire day your intellect is at prayer.*[42]

With longer prayers, in fact, there is always the danger of
distraction, because concentration quickly flags or, worse,
because the demons sow their weeds in among them.[43] As
for their content, these little prayers are quite biblical in their
inspiration. They transform the Word of God that has been
heard into a personal prayer or else simply adopt it as it is.

*Now when you stand in prayer, you should ask to be freed from
the "old man",*[44] *or say the Our Father, or both together,*[45] *and
then sit down to your handwork.*[46]

~

It should not be difficult for anyone who wants to "pray
in truth" to start from these very simple principles and de-
velop his own *personal* "method", which takes into account
the circumstances of his own life: principally the nature of his
work. For upon closer inspection one sees that these Desert
Fathers were not conducting a life of prayer *alongside* the rest
of their life, but rather worked, like any other man, so as
to make a living, and also took six hours of rest at night.
Their *prayer life is identical with their daily life*, permeates it
completely, and ultimately leads to the point at which the
spirit "is at prayer throughout the whole day". External circumstances and "disturbances" such as conversations, for
example, no longer make any difference.

[42] Barsanuphios and John, *Epistula* 143.
[43] Cassian, *Conlationes* IX, 36; similarly Augustine, *Epistula* CXXX,
20, cited below, p. 113.
[44] Cf. Eph 4:22; Col 3:9.
[45] Barsanuphios and John, *Epistula* 176.
[46] Ibid., 143.

*The brothers made the following report: "Once we went to visit
the elders, and after we had said the customary prayers and greeted
one another, we sat down. After our conversation we asked to recite
a prayer, since we wanted to leave. Then one of the elders said to
us: 'What? Haven't you prayed?' And we answered him: 'As we
came in, Abba, a prayer was recited, and since then we have been
conversing.' Then the elder said: 'Excuse me, brothers, but one
of the brothers who sat among us and conversed with us prayed
[meanwhile] 103 prayers.' And after he had said this, they recited
a prayer and left us."*[47]

It is easy to understand that such an activity—for which
an occasional or continual retreat into silence is certainly
very conducive but not at all essential—eventually brings the
spirit, by the grace of God, into a "state of prayer", in which
all idle wandering of the thoughts stops and the mind "stands
fast", with its "eyes" turned unceasingly toward God. Evagrius in one passage defines this desired "state" as follows:

*The state of prayer is a passionless disposition, which snatches the
wisdom-loving (φιλοσόφον), spiritualized intellect on high in an
extreme loving desire (ἔρωτι).*[48]

As the expression "being snatched away" clearly indicates, man's activity has reached its goal here, and God himself, namely, the Son and the Spirit, is active from there
on. "Prayer" is now no longer a particular act of our mind
among other activities, one that therefore necessarily has
temporal limitations, but is rather as spontaneous and natural as breathing, because it is "the activity of the mind that
corresponds to its worth".[49]

*Breathe Christ at all times,
and believe in him,*

[47] Nau 280.
[48] Evagrius, *De Oratione* 53.
[49] Ibid., 84.

the dying Anthony advised his disciples.[50] Prayer is the spiritual breath of the soul, the true life that is proper to it.

⁓

This ideal of continually remaining in prayer, which might seem "typically monastic" to us today,[51] is in reality much older than monasticism and is one of those "original, unwritten traditions" that the Fathers of the Church traced back to the apostles themselves. Clement of Alexandria already wrote about the true "gnostic", whose "whole life is a prayer and a conversation with God".[52]

> He prays, though, in all situations, whether he is taking a walk or with company or is resting or reading or beginning a task requiring thought. And when in the very "chamber" of his soul he harbors just one thought and "with sighs too deep for words"[53] "invokes the Father",[54] who is already present while he is still speaking.[55]

The early monks did nothing more than give to this ideal a definite form, which in its simplicity is accessible to anyone who seriously wants it. For *every* "soul" is by its very nature inclined "to praise the Lord".

> "Let everything that breathes praise the LORD!"
> If the "light of the Lord" is, according to Solomon, "the breath of man", then every rational nature that breathes in this "light" should praise the Lord.[56]

⁓

---

[50] Athanasius, *Vita Antonii* 91, 3 (Bartelink).
[51] After all, Cassian, *Conlationes* IX, 2 describes it as "the single goal of the monk and the perfection of the heart".
[52] Clement of Alexandria, *Stromata* VII, 73, 1.
[53] Rom 8:26.
[54] 1 Pet 1:17.
[55] Clement of Alexandria, *Stromata* VII, 49, 7.
[56] Evagrius, *In Ps. 150:6ι*. Citing Prov 20:27.

3. *"Lord, have mercy on me!"* (Ps 40:5)

It has perhaps seemed remarkable to many a reader of the *The Way of a Pilgrim* that the traditional formula for the perpetual prayer of the heart goes: "Lord Jesus Christ, have mercy on me, a sinner." He may have been surprised that this centerpiece of the hesychastic tradition in the Eastern Church is actually a sort of *penitential prayer*. Anyone who has read the chapter about the tears of *metanoia*, though, will not be so surprised. Rather, it will seem to him quite consistent that the Fathers finally agreed upon this formula, which we do not hear about at all in the early period of monasticism. For it reflects perfectly that *spirit* which from the beginning inspired the Fathers in their endeavors.

~

The custom of regularly saying prayers in the form of very short invocations goes back to the beginnings of monasticism in Egypt. It was known very early outside of Egypt as well, in any case from hearsay, as Augustine testifies.

> It is said that the brothers in Egypt have certain oft-repeated prayers, which are nevertheless extremely short and are hurled quickly like spears, so that the vigilantly maintained intention, which more than anything else is necessary to the one who prays, might not diminish and become dull through tarrying too long.[57]

These prayers resembling "spear thrusts" (*quodam modo iaculatas*), to which our "ejaculations" can be traced back, are already mentioned by Evagrius in numerous writings of his as an exercise that is obviously known to all. They should be said "frequently", "uninterruptedly", and "unceasingly", while remaining "short" and "to the point", to

---

[57] Augustine, *Epistula* CXXX, 20 *ad Probam* (Goldzieher III, p. 62).

mention only a few of the many synonyms that he uses in
this connection.

> During a time of temptations of that sort, make use of short and
> persistent prayer.[58]

He is referring to the demonic temptations mentioned
in the previous chapter (*De Oratione* 97), which try to ruin
"pure prayer". In that passage Evagrius gives an example of
such "short prayers":

> "I will fear no evils,
>   for you are at my side."

It is a question, then, of a short *psalm verse*.[59] As the following
remark, "and similar [texts of this sort]" tells us, the choice
was left completely to the person praying. Obviously Evagrius does not know of any fixed formula. John Cassian, on
the other hand, a contemporary of Evagrius, learned from
his Egyptian masters to use verse 2 of Psalm 69 as an ejac-
ulation most suitable for all situations in life.[60]

> O God, come to my assistance,
>   O LORD, make haste to help me!"

In other passages, the fathers almost always recommend
Scripture verses.

> One of the Fathers told the story: "In the Cellia there was a
> certain zealous elder who wore only a mat made of rushes. He
> went to visit Abba Ammonas, who, when he saw him wearing
> the mat of rushes, said to him: 'That is of no use to you!' Then
> the elder asked him: 'Three thoughts trouble me: Should I remain
> in the desert, or go abroad where no one knows me, or should I

[58] Evagrius, *De Oratione* 98.
[59] Ps 22:4.
[60] Cassian, *Conlationes* X, 10 (Petschenig).

*shut myself up in a cell and have no dealings with anyone and
eat only every other day?' Then Abba Ammonas said to him:
'None of these three things is fitting for you to do. Sit rather in
your cell, eat a little each day, and have at all times the words of
the tax collector in your heart, and you can be saved.'* "[61]

What is meant are the words, "God, be merciful to me, a
sinner",[62] a free rendering of Psalm 78:9. Ammonas is a disciple of Anthony the Great himself. In the latter's life, penned
by Athanasius the Great, we read not only that this "first
of the anchorites" (as Evagrius called him) "prayed unceasingly"[63] but also that he parried the vehement temptations
of the demons with short psalm verses.[64] Another disciple
of Anthony is Makarios the Egyptian, Evagrius' teacher, of
whom the following saying is handed down.

*Some of them asked Abba Makarios: "How should we pray?"
The elder answered them: "It is not necessary to 'rattle on,'[65]
but one has only to stretch out one's hands and say, 'Lord, as
you will'[66] and as 'you know',[67] 'have mercy on me!'[68] On the
other hand, if a battle is impending, pray, 'Lord, help me!'[69] He
himself knows what is necessary and treats us with mercy."[70]*

With this simple "Lord, help me!" the Canaanite woman,
an "unclean heathen", overcame Jesus' initial hesitation.

[61] Ammonas 4.
[62] Lk 18:13.
[63] Athanasius, *Vita Antonii* 3, 6 (Bartelink).
[64] Ibid., 13, 7 and 39, 3, 5.
[65] Mt 6:7.
[66] Cf. Mt 6:10.
[67] Cf. Mt 6:8.
[68] Ps 40:5.
[69] Mt 15:25.
[70] Makarios the Great 19.

As these few examples show, there is an uninterrupted tradition of the "brothers in Egypt" (Augustine) that goes back to Anthony the Great himself—and reaches farther beyond him to the time of Christ, as we will see.

~

A survey of the scattered texts attesting to such "ejaculatory prayers" that have been handed down to us shows that, whatever the differences in form, they all have a common spirit. They are all in all *cries for help of the man who is assailed.* "O God, be gracious to me, a sinner."[71] "Lord, have mercy on me." "Lord, help me!"[72] "Son of God, help me!"[73] "Son of God, have mercy on me."[74] "Lord, save me from the evil one!"[75]

Hence we understand what Evagrius means when he recommends "praying, not like the Pharisee, but like the tax collector",[76] namely, like that tax collector in the Gospel who acknowledged from the depths of his heart (note how he beat his breast) that he was a sinner, whose only hope was divine forgiveness.[77]

The spirit common to all of these ejaculatory prayers is the *spirit of metanoia*, of remorse, conversion, and repentance. Precisely that spirit, then, which alone is capable of accepting the "glad tidings" of "reconciliation in Christ".[78]

---

[71] Ammonas 4.
[72] Makarios the Great 19.
[73] Nau 167.
[74] Nau 184.
[75] Nau 574.
[76] Evagrius, *De Oratione* 102.
[77] Lk 18:10–14.
[78] Cf. 2 Cor 5:18–20.

> *The time is fulfilled and*
> *the kingdom of God is at hand.*
> *Repent and*
> *believe in the gospel.*[79]

Without "conversion" (μετάνοια) there is no faith; without faith there is no share in the gospel of reconciliation. For this reason the sermons of the apostles, which Luke has preserved for us in his Acts of the Apostles, almost without exception end with this call for "conversion".[80] This metanoia, however, is not a single act, but rather a life-long process. The "spirit of repentance", that is, *humility* that comes from the heart, is not attained once and for all. A lifetime is not sufficient to "learn" from Christ this essential feature, which, as he himself tells us, is his distinguishing characteristic.[81] The practice of repeating over and over again—audibly or in one's heart—this "supplication" (which was discussed in the previous chapter), in the spirit of the remorseful tax collector, is one of the best means of vigilantly maintaining an interior desire for genuine metanoia.

∼

Probably from the very beginning the short ejaculatory prayers were directed almost without exception to *Christ*, even though at first this is not always explicitly stated, since we are dealing in most cases with psalm verses. In calling on the "Lord" this goes without saying from the start; after all, the profession of Christ as *Kyrios* is the most ancient Christian creed.[82] But "Christ", for the first Christians, is

[79] Mk 1:15.
[80] Cf. Acts 2:38; 3:19; 5:31; 17:30.
[81] Mt 11:29.
[82] Acts 2:36.

practically synonymous with "Son of God".[83] Moreover the
Son is also called "God" directly: "My Lord and my God".
With this profession Thomas puts his faith in the Risen One
into words.[84] Hence it is no surprise that Evagrius, in his little prayer composed of psalm verses, changes the invocation
"Lord, Lord" first into "Lord, Christ" and then afterward
applies the words "God and protector" also to Christ as a
matter of course.

> *Lord, Christ,*
> *the strength of my salvation,*[85]
> *incline thy ear to me,*
> *make haste to rescue me!*
> *Be for me God and protector,*
> *a place of refuge*
> *to save me.*[86]

The formula that later became usual, "Lord, Jesus Christ,
have mercy on me", merely says explicitly what was meant
implicitly from the very beginning, namely, that "there is no
other name under heaven given among men by which we
must be saved",[87] except the Name of Jesus Christ. Therefore it is with good reason that the Fathers later gave particular emphasis to this salutary affirmation of "Jesus the
Christ"—to the extent of developing a full-fledged mysticism of the Name of Jesus. For the person who prays with a
"supplication" consciously takes his place among the blind
and the lame, and so on, who cried out to Jesus for help
during his life on earth. They did this in a way that is in

[83] Cf. Lk 4:41; Jn 20:31.
[84] Jn 20:28.
[85] Ps 139:8.
[86] Evagrius, *Mal. cog.* 34, 19–22 (Géhin-Guillaumont; PG 40, 1241 B).
Citing Ps 30:3.
[87] Acts 4:12.

fact appropriate only when one is turning to God—and thus they demonstrated more clearly than by any verbal profession their faith in the Divine Sonship of the Redeemer.

The profession that Jesus Christ is Lord, which is formulated in the first part of the so-called Jesus Prayer, is inseparable from the petition of the second part. If anyone thinks that from a certain moment on he no longer needs this second part, *metanoia*, let him recall what Evagrius said about tears . . .

~

The Lord taught us "to pray at all times". He also warned us, though, about the pagan practice of "rattling on", of "heaping up empty phrases",[88] The Fathers took this admonition very much to heart. Clement of Alexandria already said about the true gnostic:

> *While praying aloud, though, he does not use many words, since he has also learned from the Lord what he must pray for.[89] Therefore he will pray "in every place",[90] but not in public in plain view of everyone.[91]*

Evagrius, who made this ideal of the true Christian gnostic entirely his own and integrated it into the spirituality of monasticism, elaborates further on this thought.

> *The worth of one's prayer is not merely a question of quantity but of quality. This is made clear by the "two men [who] went*

---

[88] Mt 6:7.
[89] What is meant is the Our Father (Mt 6:9–13).
[90] 1 Tim 2:8.
[91] Clement of Alexandria, *Stromata* VII, 49, 6.

*up to the temple"[92] and furthermore by the saying, "In praying
do not heap up empty phrases," and so on.[93]*

Evagrius himself said one hundred prayers a day, so he
certainly had nothing against "quantity". It is part of the
"practical way" of prayer, which cannot make progress without practice and therefore repetition. Nevertheless, just as
the "letter" cannot exist at all without the "spirit" or the
"meaning", in the same way mere quantity does not yet
make prayer "praiseworthy", that is, pleasing to God, without the corresponding inner "quality", its Christian content,
as the Lord himself has taught us.[94]

The torrent of words poured forth by the virtuous but
self-righteous Pharisee is worthless in comparison to the few
words of the tax collector, who is burdened with sins but
remorseful. Just as worthless are the empty phrases heaped
up by the pagans who "rattle on", who act as though God
did not know what man needs,[95] in comparison to the few,
confident words of the Our Father. Therefore, when asked
which "prayer" one should say, the Fathers answer, as we
have seen, almost without exception, by referring to the
Lord's Prayer.[96]

In the little ejaculatory prayers, which anyone can say effortlessly and in all circumstances, which even in the presence of others can be said "mentally", and also in the Our
Father when it is recited audibly and devoutly "in one's

---

[92] That is, the Pharisee and the tax collector; cf. Lk 18:10.

[93] Evagrius, *De Oratione* 151.

[94] The conclusion of the chapter ("and so on") indicates that Evagrius has the Our Father in mind as an example of correct prayer!

[95] Mt 6:8.

[96] The words of the Our Father are, as it were, the red thread running
through Evagrius' work *On prayer.* Cf. Bunge, *Geistgebet*, pp. 44ff.

room", the Fathers have found a way of combining "quantity" and "quality", that is, of praying "at all times" and "unceasingly" without falling into mindless prattle.

~

One final point. Paul taught the Thessalonians not only to "pray without ceasing"; he added that they should "give thanks in all circumstances".[97] The spirit of metanoia in the prayer of the heart is in fact entirely compatible with *thanksgiving* for every good thing that the Lord does for us. Therefore one of Evagrius' "definitions" of prayer runs:

> *Prayer is a fruit of joy and of thanksgiving.*[98]

The old Ethiopian tradition gave a particular form to the perpetual prayer of the heart, which in a uniquely simple way combines petition and thanksgiving into one.

> *Abba Paulos the Cenobite said: "When you are staying among the brothers, work, learn by heart, slowly lift your eyes to heaven, and speak from the depths of your heart to the Lord: Jesus, have mercy on me! Jesus, help me! I praise you, my God!' "*[99]

It is also this same Ethiopian tradition that calls to mind the true *theological horizon* of all prayer: the eschatological waiting for the Parousia of the Lord, his second coming "in the glory of the Father with the holy angels."[100]

> *A brother said to me: "See, this is what waiting for the Lord consists of. Your heart is turned toward the Lord while you cry*

[97] 1 Thess 5:18.
[98] Evagrius, *De Oratione* 15.
[99] Eth. Coll. 13, 42; cf. Lucien Regnault, *Les Sentences des Pères du désert, nouveau recueil* (Solesmes), pp. 298–99.
[100] Mk 8:38.

out, Jesus, have mercy on me! Jesus, help me! I praise you at all times, my living God! And you slowly lift your eyes while saying these words to the Lord in your heart.[101]

~

4. *"Hear, O LORD, when I cry aloud"* (Ps 26:7)

We are used to hearing public prayers being offered up in the name of the congregation in an audible voice by a priest or a so-called "presider". On the other hand, almost everyone prays silently when alone. Men in biblical times, in contrast, not only *read* in an undertone (*sotto voce*), that is, they actually read aloud to themselves, but they also *meditated* and even *prayed* as a rule in an audible voice as well. Therefore we find again and again in the psalms, for instance, expressions like: "Hear the voice of my supplication."[102] Furthermore, the psalmist "cries aloud to the LORD,"[103] and we even hear "his words" and "the sound of his cry".[104]

This is evidently the rule, not the exception. When Hannah, silent with grief, prayed in the temple of Shiloh, only moving her lips without allowing her voice to be heard, Eli the priest concluded that she must be drunk . . .[105]

Hence the prayers handed down to us in the New Testament, and even more plentifully in the writings of the Fathers, which are said to have been recited on one occasion or another, cannot simply be dismissed as mere poetic inventions. For the man of antiquity it was self-evident that

[101] Eth. Coll. 13, 26 (Regnault, *Nouveau recueil*, p. 293).
[102] Ps 27:2 passim.
[103] Ps 3:5 and many other verses.
[104] Ps 5:2; 17:7, etc.
[105] 1 Sam 1:12ff.

such freely formulated prayers were said for all to hear and thus could also be handed down as "maxims". Indeed, the sayings of the Desert Fathers, too, are full of such prayers, some of which are very short and simple, while others are quite extensive; all of them, at any rate, are spontaneous.

> The story is told of Abba Makarios the Great that he visited a brother in the skete every day for four months and did not once find him idle. When he visited him yet again and remained outside standing at the door, he heard him saying tearfully: "Lord, do your ears not hear me crying out to you? Have mercy on me on account of my sins, for I do not grow weary of calling to you for help."[106]

Such a direct expression of emotions might seem strange to modern man, as something not at all in keeping with his ideas of "prayer" and "meditation". And yet the spiritual Fathers—including those in the Christian East down to this day—teach that one should recite even the *prayer of the heart* in an undertone, at least at the beginning and for a certain time, that is, until it has become truly united with one's heartbeat. For they knew that this, as in the case of reading or "meditating" in an undertone, is an excellent means of bringing *distractions* under control, which are otherwise so difficult to overcome.

> When the intellect wanders, then reading, watching, and prayer bring it to a standstill.[107]

Hearing one's own voice makes it easier to concentrate on the words of Scripture, of the psalms, or of the prayer, just as the beads of the rosary slipping through the fingers, in another way, focus the attention. Someone who wants to

---

[106] Nau 16.
[107] Evagrius, *Praktikos* 15.

learn a text by heart will do so, even today, by reciting it to himself aloud or in an undertone. For even though prayer in and of itself is a purely spiritual phenomenon, the body must nevertheless be able to make its contribution to it. This will be discussed in detail in the chapter on gestures in prayer.

～

The man of biblical times, nevertheless, would hardly have been thinking about this practical benefit of praying out loud or *sotto voce* when he "cried aloud to the LORD." His "loud cries" were, instead, the expression of the *immediacy* of the relationship, which modern man to a great extent has lost sight of. The Lord to whom he calls is, after all, no purely abstract principle like the "God of the philosophers"; neither is he the "distant God" of the Gnostics, but rather the "living God", who of his own accord reveals himself to man, speaks to him, and also demands that he for his part turn to him.

> *Call upon me in the day of trouble*
> *and I will deliver you*
> *and you shall glorify me.*[108]
> *For the LORD is near to all who call upon him,*
> *to all who call upon him in truth.*[109]

This is, indeed, in stark contrast to the idols, who have mouths but cannot speak, eyes but cannot see, ears and do not hear . . .[110] "God, who is near", however, "hears the voice of my supplication."[111] Furthermore he alone pos-

---

[108] Ps 49:15.
[109] Ps 144:18.
[110] Ps 113:13f.
[111] Ps 27:2.

sesses, in the true sense of the word, a "face", which is not merely a silver or golden mask, as in the case of something "made by human hands". Therefore the one who prays also "seeks" this "face of God"[112] and asks him to "let his face shine upon him",[113] so that he may be "saved".[114]

These and other very graphic ways of speaking about God are much more than mere poetic metaphors. The more spiritualized the image of God in the Old Covenant becomes, the more "anthropomorphic"—having a human form—speech about God can and must be, if the relationship with God is not to evaporate into impersonal abstractions. The Old Testament prophets are the most often cited examples of this seemingly paradoxical development. Their God is, as John would later say, entirely "spirit",[115] in sharp contrast to all the pagan reification of the divine. For precisely this reason, though, they can dare to speak of him in an unprecedented, concretely anthropomorphic way.

In the Incarnation of the Word, this personal being of God, his being present *for us* as well, has transcended all imaginable limitations. His nearness in the Son is a light that blinds the unbeliever with its radiance. Only to the believer does the Son grant access to the "hidden Father"; he even makes it possible for the believer to call him by the familiar name of "Abba—dear Father", as only a child would dare to address his father who is physically present.

Is there any reason why the believer not speak audibly to this God who is absolutely *present*, that is, when he is in his room with him alone or thinks that he is alone? Yes, prayer is a time to be on guard against all sorts of vanity. Therefore,

[112] Ps 26:8.
[113] Ps 30:17.
[114] Ps 79:4, 8, 20.
[115] Jn 4:24.

during the "prayer" that followed each of the twelve psalms of the morning and evening office, the monks therefore remained "in perfect silence", as John Cassian reports from first-hand observation.[116] What matters in the final analysis, though, is taught by the following saying of Bishop Epiphanius of Salamis on the isle of Cyprus.

> He himself said: "The Canaanite woman cried out and was heard,[117] and the woman with the hemorrhage remained silent and was called blessed.[118] The Pharisee called [in an audible voice] and was condemned, while the tax collector did not even open his mouth and was heard."[119]

Ultimately it does not depend on whether we pray aloud or silently—be it "together with others or alone by ourselves"—but instead on whether we pray "in a routine way" or "with feeling", as Evagrius says.[120]

> The feeling (αἴσθησις) that accompanies prayer is [a certain] seriousness, combined with reverence, contrition, and grief of soul in acknowledging one's failings "with loud sighs".[121]

~

Finally, we should not leave unmentioned another reason for reciting the psalms aloud and, under certain circumstances, for praying out loud as well—a reason that may at first seem strange to modern man until he has personally experienced the truth of it. God is not the only one to hear the voice of the person praying; the *demons* hear it, too!

---

[116] Cassian, *De Institutis* II, 8 (Petschenig).
[117] Mt 15:21ff.
[118] Mt 9:20f.
[119] Epiphanius 6. Citing Lk 18:9ff.
[120] Evagrius, *De Oratione* 42.
[121] Ibid., 43. Citing Rom 8:26.

Question: *When I pray or recite psalms and because of the hardness of my heart am not conscious of the meaning of what is said, what good does it do me then?*

Answer: *Even if you are not conscious [of the meaning], the demons are still conscious of it, and they hear and tremble! Therefore do not stop reciting psalms and praying, and by and by your hardness of heart will be alleviated with God's help.*[122]

The demons are reduced to "trembling" especially by those psalm verses that speak about the "enemies" and their destruction by the Lord, for example, all of the "imprecatory psalms" that present such great difficulties for modern sensibilities, because their cursing seems to be irreconcilable with the spirit of the gospel. The Fathers, who were well aware "that the just man is not cursing but praying,"[123] spiritualized these texts as a matter of course and related them to the "enemies" of the human race par excellence, the demons. The latter understood this quite well and fear it, which is why they sometimes even attempt to turn this weapon back on the one who wields it, as Evagrius assures us.

I have also come to recognize demons who compel us to recite "psalms and spiritual songs"[124] *in which precisely those commandments are found which we—deceived [by them]—have transgressed, in order to mock us, when they hear it, as men "who preach and do not practice".*[125] *Therefore David, too, says:*[126] *"Let not the godless exult over me."*[127]

The same reasons that the Fathers had for praying and especially for reciting psalms aloud in this battle, not only

---

[122] Barsanuphios and John, *Epistula* 711, cf. 429.
[123] Evagrius, *In Ps. 108:9* ξ, with a reference to Rom 12:14.
[124] Col 3:16.
[125] Mt 23:3.
[126] The citation conflates Ps 118:122 and Ps 24:2.
[127] Evagrius, *In Ps. 136:3* β.

against evil but against the evil one, which they understood quite concretely, impelled them also to pray silently under certain circumstances, as we will now see.

～

5. *"A time to keep silence and a time to speak"* (Eccles 3:7)

As much as the Fathers liked to read, recite psalms, meditate, and even pray out loud, or at least in an audible voice, this was by no means a rule to which they were bound. Tertullian recommends praying at all times "in a lowered voice", since God is no "hearer of voices, but of hearts". Prayer that is too loud only disturbs the neighbors or, worse still, is tantamount to praying on the street corners[128] and thus is essentially nothing more than that vain display which Christ expressly forbade his disciples to make.[129] Clement of Alexandria also makes a statement along these lines.

> *Hence prayer is, to venture an audacious expression, a conversation with God. Therefore if we speak to him only in a whisper or silently, without even opening our lips, we still call out to him aloud in our hearts; for God continuously hears the inner voice of our heart.*[130]

God *alone* hears this voice of the heart, in fact, since he alone "knows the hearts of all men".[131] In contrast, not only our fellow men hear our bodily voice, but also the demons, as we have seen. It makes sense, therefore, to conceal from them carefully the content of our intimate conversation with God.

[128] Tertullian, *De Oratione* 17.
[129] Mt 6:5ff.
[130] Clement of Alexandria, *Stromata* VII, 39, 6.
[131] Acts 1:24.

*We pray "in secret" when we make our petitions known to God
alone in our heart and with a watchful mind, in such manner
that the hostile powers cannot even tell what sort of petition it is.
Therefore one should pray in the most profound silence, not only
so as to avoid distracting the brothers around us by our whispering
and calling, or disturbing the sentiments of those who are at prayer,
but also so that the purpose of our petition might remain hidden
from our enemies themselves, who lie in wait for us especially when
we pray. In this way, then, we fulfill the commandment: "Guard
the doors of your mouth from her who lies in your bosom."*[132]

Of course, what the adversaries ought to hear are the
words of the psalms, which are inspired by the Holy Spirit
and insistently announce their destruction. That will scare
them and put them to flight. This is what Evagrius has in
mind when he advises:

*Do not pray, when you are being tempted, until you have said
a few words in anger against the one who is oppressing you. Because your soul has been assailed by thoughts, it follows that your
prayer, too, is not pure when it is offered. Nevertheless, if in fury
you say something against them, you thwart and destroy the mental images of the adversary. Indeed, anger usually has this effect
even upon good mental images.*[133]

The content of our intimate conversation with God, on
the other hand, ought to remain hidden from the demons;
otherwise they could poison it bit by bit with their temptations.

~

---

[132] Cassian, *Conlationes* IX, 35. Citing Mic 7:5 (Vulgate).
[133] Evagrius, *Praktikos* 42.

Nevertheless, praying aloud disturbs not only the neighbors but, under certain circumstances, the one praying, too. Instead of promoting recollection, it can also hinder it. Indeed, not only can my own voice be distracting (that would be the least of my problems). What proves to be much more distracting and troublesome over time are my *own words and thoughts*, which I necessarily make use of while praying. Although this goes beyond our actual subject, we still ought to speak briefly here about that *silence of the heart* as well, which is the ultimate goal of all our efforts.

In his work *On Prayer*, Evagrius adopts the beautiful definition of prayer given by Clement of Alexandria and in his own way makes it more profound. Prayer is a "conversation (ὁμιλία) with God", says Clement. Evagrius adds: "a conversation of the intellect with God *without any mediation whatsoever*".[134] This "true prayer" thus takes place *immediately*; as we would say today, it is a "personal" encounter between God and man.

Standing in the way of this desired immediacy, nevertheless, are not only our voices and our words but also and above all our "mental images" (νοήματα), insofar as they represent a "mediation" between us and God. This means not only the passionate, sinful "thoughts"[135] but *all* thoughts whatsoever about created things, or even about God himself, be they ever so sublime, since they hold a person bound to human concerns.[136] In a word, man must "cast aside *all* mental images"[137] if he wants to "pray in truth". This "withdrawal" is a step-by-step process corresponding to the ascent in the

---

[134] Evagrius, *De Oratione* 3.

[135] Ibid., 55.

[136] Ibid., 56–58.

[137] Evagrius, *Skemmata* 2 (J. Muyldermans, *Evagriana* [Paris, 1931], p. 374).

spiritual life, not a "technique" to be acquired somehow, as one often encounters in many non-Christian methods of "meditation". Man, to be sure, does his share in this, but he cannot accomplish this "transcendence" by his own power, because the destination, God, is a "Person" who inclines himself to man with absolute freedom.[138]

> *The intellect does not contemplate the "place of God"[139] within itself, unless it goes beyond all thoughts about created things. However it does not go beyond them unless it sets aside the passions, which bind him to sensible things through his thoughts.*
>
> *Now it will set aside the passions through the virtues; mere thoughts,[140] on the other hand, he will set aside through spiritual contemplation. This, in turn, [he will set aside] when that light begins to shine for him which represents during the time of prayer the "place of God".[141]*

The created spirit sees this "light of the Holy Trinity" —the sign of God's personal presence—not outside itself, but rather "within itself", as it is stated explicitly, namely in that intelligible "mirror" which he himself is, by virtue of being created "in the image of God".[142]

~

[138] Cf. Evagrius, *Epistula* 29, 3. "Illumination" in Christian mysticism is always the free, completely gratuitous [*unverfügbar* = not to be disposed of at will by the recipient] *self-revelation* of the triune God.

[139] Cf. Ex 24:10 (the place where God's feet stood).

[140] Meant here is the pure content of knowledge, which neither "forms" nor "leaves an imprint on" our mind. Cf. *Mal. cog.* 41, 1–3 (Géhin-Guillaumont; PG 79, 1228 C).

[141] Evagrius, *Mal cog.* 40 (Géhin-Guillaumont; PG 40, 1244 A/B).

[142] Cf. Evagrius, *Kephalaia Gnostika* II, 1 (Guillaumont).

Should this unusual grace of entering the mysterious "place of prayer"[143] be granted to anyone, then it is fitting that he adapt his own activity to this absolutely new thing. Indeed, he actually does this quite spontaneously, as Diadochos of Photike teaches.

> *When the soul finds itself amidst the fullness of its natural fruits, then it recites the psalmody with an even stronger voice and desires, more than anything else, to pray aloud. When, however, the Holy Spirit works within it, then it recites the psalms very gently and lovingly and prays in the heart alone.*
>
> *The first state is followed by a joy that is bound up with mental imagery; the second, by spiritual tears and thereafter a certain joy in the heart that loves silence. For being mindful [of God], which maintains its warmth through the moderation of the voice, enables the heart to bring forth tearful, very gentle thoughts.*[144]

The masters of the spiritual life expressly warn against disturbing this "visitation of the Holy Spirit"[145] by stubbornly clinging to one's own activity or to any self-imposed "rule". At this moment the only valid law is that of "the freedom of the children of God", as the East-Syrian mystic Joseph Hazzaya teaches.

> *Close all the doors of your cell, enter the inner room, and sit down in darkness and seclusion in a place where you do not even hear the song of a bird. Then when the hour for the Divine Office comes, beware, do not stand up, lest you be like a child that in its ignorance exchanges a talent of gold for a fig that sweetens its gums for an instant. But you, like a wise merchant, once you have discovered the "pearl of great price",[146] do not exchange this for contemptible things that you find before you at all times, lest you*

---

[143] Evagrius, *De Oratione* 57 and *passim*.
[144] Diadochos of Photike, c. LXXIII (des Places).
[145] Evagrius, *De Oratione* 70.
[146] Mt 13:46.

end as did that people which went forth from Egypt and which despised the food of the spiritual manna and craved the loathsome food of the Egyptians.[147]

This freedom even from the Divine Office, which for monks is otherwise absolutely obligatory, is valid as long as this divine light shines upon the one who is praying. As soon as he departs from this "place", and depart he must, he also returns in all humility and fidelity to his usual activities again.[148]

~

But not only the lips have to be silent at the "place of prayer"! "Silent worship of the ineffable"[149] also means, above all, silence of the "heart", as we have seen, hence the silence of all thoughts about God. Paradoxically, though, this adoring silence is not the ultimate thing, as that same East-Syrian Father cited above teaches. For if the Holy Ghost leads man further into the light of the Holy Trinity, there bursts forth in him finally a stream of mysterious "speech", which day and night never again runs dry.[150] Evagrius describes this astonishing experience in the following words:

He who "prays in spirit and in truth"[151] *no longer honors the Creator from the creatures, but rather praises [God] with hymns from within Himself.*[152]

---

[147] Joseph Hazzaya, p. 153. With reference to Num 11:5–6.
[148] Ibid., p. 159.
[149] Evagrius, *Gnostikos* 41 (Guillaumont).
[150] Joseph Hazzaya (Joseph the Visionary), pp. 156ff.
[151] Jn 4:23.
[152] Evagrius, *De Oratione* 60.

This, finally, is that "conversation with God *without any mediation whatsoever*" which was spoken of earlier. For creatures, however exalted they may be, are still always things [intervening and] mediating between us and God. "Spirit and truth", though, that is to say, according to the Evagrian interpretation of John 4:23, the Persons of the Holy Spirit and of the only begotten Son,[153] are not creatures but rather "God from God", as the Creed of the Second Ecumenical Council [the Council of Constantinople] (381) teaches.

One who through "true" and "spiritual" prayer has become a "theologian" in the strict sense of the word,[154] therefore, praises the *Father* at the highest level of prayer "without any mediation whatsoever"—neither of a creature nor of a mental representation or contemplation—immediately, *through the Spirit and the Son*! He has become a "theologian", because now he no longer speaks *about* God from hearsay, but rather bears witness *to* the Holy Trinity on the basis of his intimate familiarity.[155]

If "eternal life" consists in the fact that we "know [the Father,] the only true God and Jesus Christ whom [he has] sent",[156] then the prayer "in spirit and in truth" is a genuine foretaste of this eschatological blessedness.

[153] Ibid., 59.
[154] Ibid., 61.
[155] Cf. Evagrius, *Ad Monachos* 120 (Gressmann).
[156] Jn 17:3.

Chapter IV

Prayer Gestures

Today one often hears the reproach that Christianity—
supposedly "hostile toward the body"—assigns too little
importance to the body in the spiritual life. One misses all
of those finely honed "methods" of sitting, breathing, and
so on, which are so characteristic of the religions of the Far
East. There is a longing to get away from the emphasis on
"the head" in the spiritual life and to pray instead "with the
body".

The reproach is based in part on a misunderstanding, as
though the Christian "methods" had to be absolutely of the
same sort as those of the non-Christian religions, and in part
on ignorance. "I was astonished . . . at all that the ancients
already knew and wondered how much of it their descen-
dants forgot." This exclamation of surprise, which escaped
from F. J. Dölger while he was reading a book from the
beginning of the seventeenth century,[1] best describes the
gradual neglect of all that the Fathers once knew—and *put
into practice*. For our spiritual life—in the West—has by no
means always been so devoid of prayer gestures and the like
as is unfortunately the case today. All the gestures that the
East-Syrian mystic Joseph Busnaya (d. 979) once enumer-
ated, and which we will discuss in detail in the following

[1] F. J. Dölger, *Beiträge zur Geschichte des Kreuzzeichens I*, JbAC 1
(1958), p. 5.

chapter, were at one time the common property of East and West.

> *The bows, the stretching out [of the hands] during the Divine Office, the continual genuflections during prayer, confer on the monk, during the constant standing of the Office in the presence of God, humbling and abasement of the mind, warmth of the heart, purification of the body, ardor of the soul, and diligence in thought. For without prostrations, bows, stretching out the hands, and genuflections, the Office of the brothers will be routine, cold, and shallow, as will be the prayers said during it.*
>
> *Devote yourself therefore to these things, my son, with all your strength, forcefully, ardently, and courageously, so that your offering might be pleasing to God.*[2]

Liturgical scholars know quite well that these words could also have been written by a Western author from the Middle Ages. Recall, for example, the "Nine Ways of Prayer of Saint Dominic". One can recognize on an illustrated manuscript many different gestures, including deep bows, prostrations (*venia*), genuflections, standing, praying with hands outstretched in the form of a cross, meditation while sitting—in each case facing a crucifix that is placed on the eastern wall of the cell.

For various reasons this entire wealth of bodily expressions has been lost bit by bit since the beginning of the second millennium, until in modern times only kneeling remained. Up to the present, indeed, the faithful knelt both during the public worship of the liturgy and also during private prayer, preferably on a *prie-dieu* or "kneeler" specially constructed for the purpose. In recent times, however, these kneelers

[2] J.-B. Chabot, "Vie du moine Youssef Bousnaya", *Revue de l'Orient Chrétien* 4 (1899): 411.

have disappeared from many churches and, with them, the custom of kneeling to pray.

Let us look at what the "original, unwritten tradition" of the Church has in store for us in the way of prayer gestures, and in what spirit the holy Fathers made use of them!

~

1. *"Rise and pray"* (Lk 22:46)

Modern man in the Western world, however much he values sports and physical activity, has become a *sedentary* creature in the spiritual life. Not only does he sit most of the time in services of public worship; he also spends his moments of private meditation comfortable and relaxed on a cushion or a small stool, in a sitting posture.

What a difference between that and the characteristic posture for prayer of men in biblical times, and also of the fathers! Not sitting in comfort, but rather *standing* at the cost of some effort is the hallmark of the one who prays. He "stands in the house of the LORD, in the courts of the house of our God"[3] and "in his holy place",[4] whether he is a self-righteous Pharisee or a remorseful tax collector who scarcely dares to stand at a distance.[5]

Hence Christ, too, as a matter of course exhorts his disciples: "Rise and pray."[6] Or he warns them not to pray like the hypocrites, who "love to stand and pray . . . at the street corners, that they may be seen by men".[7] Accordingly, Mark

[3] Ps 133:1, cf. 134:2.
[4] Ps 23:3.
[5] Lk 18:11, 13.
[6] Lk 22:46.
[7] Mt 6:5.

11:25 does not say in a general way, "When you pray", as some versions have it, but rather very definitely: "Whenever you stand praying".

~

The early Church carried on the biblical and apostolic tradition without any break.

After the meal one should get up to pray,

it says in the *Apostolic Tradition* of Hippolytus of Rome (at the beginning of the third century).[8] The reference here is to the *common prayer* after the *agape*, or convivial meal that was connected with the celebration of the Eucharist; even today Christians usually stand up to pray after eating. The Fathers and the great masters of the spiritual life, however, considered *personal prayer* to be no different in this respect.

It was also said [of Abba Arsenios] that on Saturday evening, as the Lord's day began, he let the sun set behind him and stretched out his hands to heaven in prayer, until the sun shone again in his face. Then he would sit down.[9]

Arsenios the Great, a high official of the Byzantine court before he became a strict ascetic in the Egyptian desert, was furthermore of the opinion that a monk, if he was a good fighter, should be able to do with one hour of sleep . . .[10] It should be noted that the text cited above describes the night before the *Lord's day*, which the monks—and, originally, the early Christians in general—used to spend in watching

---

[8] *Traditio Apostolica*, c. 25 (B. Botte, *La Tradition apostolique de Saint Hippolyte: Essai de reconstitution*, Liturgiewissenschaftliche Quellen und Forschungen, 39 [Münster, 1963], p. 64).

[9] Arsenios 30.

[10] Arsenios 15.

and praying, thus waiting for the return of Christ. Standing to pray, however, is the general practice. Anthony the Great learned from an angel how a monk could avoid boredom, even though he lived in continual seclusion in his cell. He *works sitting down* and gets up at regular intervals, so as *to pray while standing.*[11] The examples could be multiplied indefinitely; let one suffice here.

> *Once Abraham, the disciple of Abba Sisoes, was tempted by a demon, and the elder saw that he had given way. At that he stood up, lifted his hands up to heaven, and said, "O God, whether you will it or not, I will not let you alone until you have healed him!" And immediately he was healed.*[12]

$\sim$

The general custom of standing up to pray, naturally, does not mean that one is allowed to pray *only* while standing.

> *Still, as we emphasize, this must take place as a matter of course whenever there are no [special] circumstances; for in some circumstances it is permitted to pray even while sitting in a suitable way if one is suffering from a foot ailment that is not trifling, or else lying down on account of fever or similar illnesses; furthermore it is permitted on account of special circumstances, for example, when we travel by ship, or when the situation does not allow us to withdraw and perform our duty of praying—then it is permissible to pray even without giving the [outward] appearance of doing so.*[13]

These obvious, common-sense exceptions only prove the general rule: He who wants to pray to God normally does so standing. No different was the opinion of the masters of the spiritual life, even though one might expect that they

[11] Antonios 1.
[12] Sisoes 12.
[13] Origen, *De Oratione* XXXI, 2.

used special "methods" that were not the general custom. The only bodily posture that Evagrius, for instance, appears to know of at all in his famous *153 Chapters on Prayer* is *"standing during prayer"*.[14] All of the astonishing things that the monk participates in "during the time of prayer", including the "state of prayer" (κατάστασις προσευχῆς) itself, occur when he "stands to pray". This holds true even at the level of the Evagrian "mysticism" of prayer; the goal of all the monk's efforts, after all, is to bring "to a standstill" the intellect, which by nature is extremely mobile.[15]

A man bound in chains cannot run, nor can an intellect enslaved to the passions see the place of spiritual prayer. Indeed, it is dragged off by passionate thoughts and has no fixed place to stand.[16]

These "passionate thoughts" destroy the desired *"state of prayer"*[17] and thus prevent the one who prays "from reaching out to his Lord unswervingly and holding a conversation with him without any mediation".[18]

~

The question thus arises: Why does the man of the Bible pray while standing? Why do the Fathers also, as a rule, stand up to pray? The question is not unfounded, considering that Westerners today often do not even kneel any more to pray, and many consciously assume the most relaxed, comfortable posture they can, whereas Orthodox Christians today—in public worship at the Divine Liturgy and also in private

---

[14] Evagrius, *De Oratione* 9, 10, 29, 41, 45, 49, 105, 153.
[15] Cf. Evagrius, *Praktikos* 15.
[16] Evagrius, *De Oratione* 72.
[17] Ibid., 27.
[18] Ibid., 3.

prayer—still prefer to pray standing. The Fathers, too, gave thought to this question at a very early date.

> *Nor may anyone doubt that of the countless postures* (κατάστα-σις) *of the body, the posture with hands outstretched and eyes uplifted is to be preferred to all [the others], because one then carries in the body too, as it were, the image* (εἰκών) *of that special condition which befits the soul during prayer.*[19]

This remark of Origen is of fundamental significance and applies to all prayer methods and gestures; indeed, he mentions several of them. Between the "special condition" of the soul during prayer and the posture of the body that we then assume, there must be a *perfect correspondence*. What Tertullian says about the sacraments, about the relation between visible, corporeal actions and invisible, spiritual workings of grace, can be applied also to prayer and its gestures:

> *The body is washed so that the soul may be freed from its stains; the body is anointed, so that the soul too may be consecrated; the body is signed [with the cross], so that the soul too may be strengthened [protected]."*[20]

Like sacramental actions, methods and gestures in prayer must also be *meaningful*, that is to say, the body must *reproduce visibly* what is taking place in the soul. As it is understood in the Bible, standing to pray is the bodily expression of the profound *reverence* of the creature before the exalted majesty of its Creator, in whose presence even the angels stand.[21] For the inferior stands up to greet the superior and remains standing as long as the latter is present. Thus for example

---

[19] Origen, *De Oratione* XXXI, 2.

[20] Tertullian, *De Carnis Resurrectione* 8 (*Tertullian's Treatise on the Resurrection*, ed. and trans. Ernest Evans [London, 1960], p. 24).

[21] Lk 1:19.

Abraham stands before God when the latter speaks with him, knowing full well that he is only "dust and ashes".[22]

The outward posture, however, does not only give bodily expression to the interior attitude, it *also has an immediate effect upon this disposition*. Without the effort of standing—and of the other prayer gestures, which will be discussed later —our prayer will never attain the proper fervor, said Joseph Busnaya, but will remain "routine, cold, and shallow".

Thus there is a genuine *reciprocity* between one's internal disposition and external posture. This is the "special property" of the soul, which in the body's posture creates, so to speak, a suitable "icon" of itself, which therefore always precedes it, as Origen says in this connection. Once such a visible representation exists, though—once a suitable gesture has been formed and has become a "tradition" in the course of salvation history, then the individual cannot forgo it without harming his "interior condition". By making it his own, on the other hand, and "practicing" it diligently, he forms and strengthens within himself that same interior disposition that once created the gesture, as Joseph Busnaya teaches.

At a time when the Church is especially emphasizing and promoting the introduction of the biblical message into the different cultures that make up humanity, the obviously supratemporal meaning attributed to those external aspects of prayer will probably cause consternation for many people. Nevertheless, the Fathers evidently saw no problem with this. The testimonies, which could be multiplied *ad libitum*, date from different epochs and originate in the most varied cultural regions. Culturally conditioned differences of sensibility seem to be of no importance for either the Latin Ter-

[22] Gen 18:27, cf. 18:22.

tullian or the East-Syrian Joseph Busnaya. However much
the Fathers were ready to adopt existing customs or else to
give a Christian meaning to them, they were not willing to
renounce those special things in particular that had entered
into the history of mankind with revelation. For in Christ
there is "neither Greek nor Jew . . . neither barbarian nor
Scythian",[23] and hence all cultural barriers have been lowered. For this reason, when it comes to a conflict, biblical
tradition becomes a fearless *critique of culture* as well. Thus,
for example, the rigorist Tertullian does not want to grant
any validity at all to the heathen custom, found also among
the Christians, of sitting down after prayer.

> *If it shows disrespect to sit down in the presence of someone greatly
> feared and honored, how much more is such conduct quite irreli-
> gious in the presence of the living God, when considering the angel
> of prayer is still standing there,[24] unless we are remonstrating with
> God because the prayer has wearied us!*[25]

For the Christian, standing reverently before God in prayer
means that he is aware that in the *Person* of God he has a real
interlocutor who is most certainly present. He knows from
revelation that he himself is a created person—a truth that
he never experiences except in the encounter with the absolute Person of God, even though it may forever surpass
his comprehension.

Where this revealed knowledge of the personal nature
of God is absent, for instance in paganism, where the gods
are never anything more than personifications of impersonal

---

[23] Col 3:11.
[24] Cf. Tob 12:15; 1 Cor 11:10.
[25] Tertullian, *De Oratione* 16.

divinity, man assumes another attitude automatically. This is also true where this once-accessible knowledge disappears or evaporates into a false feeling of "inwardness". Then the person spontaneously makes things as comfortable as possible for himself whenever he devotes his attention to this "divinity". How far we have today often strayed from the spirit of Sacred Scripture and the Fathers may be illustrated by a text of Evagrius the mystic.

> *When you go to stand in prayer before God, the Almighty Creator, whose providence embraces all, why in the world do you place yourself before him so irrationally that you overlook the fear of him, which surpasses everything, and are frightened by gnats and beetles? Or have you not heard the saying, "You shall fear the LORD, your God,"*[26] *and again: "[Fear] him, before the mighty face of whom all things quake and tremble" and so on?*[27]

The one who prays must not allow anything to divert him from this reverent standing before God: neither demonic appearances, which are nothing more than bothersome "gnats and beetles",[28] nor the awareness of our own weakness and sinfulness. For the adversaries make use of these same evil thoughts, which they whisper into our ears,

> *in order to draw us away from prayer, so that we might no longer stand before the Lord nor dare to stretch out our hands to him, against whom we had such things in mind.*[29]

〜

[26] Deut 6:13.

[27] Evagrius, *De Oratione* 100. Citing the Prayer of Manasseh 4.

[28] The Fathers, in fact, regarded them as such. Cf. Makarios the Great 33 (as flies), Am 17:49 (small animals, gnats, and other vermin) (in Regnault, *Troisième recueil*, p. 177).

[29] Evagrius, *Praktikos* 46, cf. *De Oratione* 90.

2. *"Let the lifting up of my hands be before thee
   as an evening sacrifice"* (Ps 140:2)

The fundamental biblical attitude of prayer, as we have seen,
is standing before God. Yet the Fathers did not just stand
there; at the same time they also lifted up their hands to
heaven. The early Christians must have felt that this gesture of prayer—*manibus extensis*, with outstretched hands—
was so typical of them that they preferred to be portrayed as
orantes, as countless examples of early Christian iconography
testify. However, because we are dealing here with a very
common but by no means exclusively Christian gesture, we
will have to ask what particular meaning the Christians assigned to it.

~

Whereas the pagan—and also the apostate—throws himself
down to worship before an idol[30] and lifts up his hands to
this "strange god" in vain,[31] since this mute object fash-
ioned by his own hands is less capable of helping than another man would be, the believer lifts up his hands only "in
the name of God",[32] who "created heaven and earth" and
is able to do everything that he wills.[33] He does this also
"in the night" when he "cries aloud to God"[34] in his dis-
tress. He not only "lifts up" his hands; he "stretches them
out",[35] when his "soul, like a parched land,"[36] thirsts for the

[30] Ps 96:7, 105:19.
[31] Cf. Ps 43:21.
[32] Ps 62:5.
[33] Ps 113:11f.
[34] Ps 76:3.
[35] Ps 87:10.
[36] Ps 142:6.

living water of God. And because God has communicated himself to man completely in his word, in his commandments, the one who prays stretches his hands out figuratively—imploring, yearning—toward these manifestations of the divine will also, "which he loves".[37]

The gesture of lifting up one's hands in prayer, then, was customary for the man of the Bible from the very beginning,[38] and therefore Christ and the apostles also prayed accordingly. Thus Paul, for example, admonishes the faithful "in every place . . . [to] pray, lifting holy hands without anger or quarreling".[39] Such prayer, even in the Old Covenant, is a substitute for all material sacrifices. It "ascends like incense" to God, and "the lifting up of my hands" is to him "as an evening sacrifice".[40]

Like the lifting up of the eyes, which will be discussed later, stretching out one's hands is also the expression of an intimate and quite *personal relationship* of the creature with his Creator. In addition this gesture gives a *direction*, as it were, to prayer. For the one praying lifts up his hands "to heaven" as the symbolic "place" of God, or else to the temple as the place of his presence among his people in the course of salvation history.[41] Christians go even one step farther by turning, not only toward heaven, but also toward the "orient", as we have seen.

The early Fathers were well aware of the symbolic meaning of this gesture, which is so moving on a human level as well. Thus, for example, Clement of Alexandria writes at the beginning of the third century:

[37] Ps 118:48.
[38] Cf. Ex 9:29.
[39] 1 Tim 2:8.
[40] Ps 140:2.
[41] Ps 10:4.

That is why we also raise our head toward the heights [while praying] and stretch out our hands to heaven and, while reciting the concluding words of the prayer together, stand on tip-toe, in that way seeking to follow the yearning of the mind upward into the spiritual world. After we have raised our soul to the heights —a soul to which longing has lent wings[42]—*we try at the same time, through the words that we have spoken, to free the body from the earth, and we strain with all our might to reach "the sanctuary"*[43] *by despising the bonds of the flesh.*[44]

Or, to put it in Origen's words:

Nor may anyone doubt that of the countless postures of the body, the posture with hands outstretched and eyes uplifted is to be preferred to all [the others], because one then carries in the body too, as it were, the image of that special condition that befits the soul during prayer.[45]

It is often said nowadays that one must also "pray with the body", and therefore much importance is ascribed to the corresponding "techniques". What the Fathers meant, though, was something different. The body does not stand, as it were, on its own beside the soul. Rather, the two make up a perfect unity. The *whole man prays*, body and soul, whereby the body, so to speak, provides the soul with a medium through which it can make visible its "special condition"—in this case its striving for God, which is invisible in and of itself. And this is no insignificant thing, as we shall see, because this "embodiment" keeps the inner disposition from evaporating into something insubstantial.

$\sim$

[42] Cf. Ps 54:7.
[43] Cf. Ps 133:2; Heb 9:24f.
[44] Clement of Alexandria, *Stromata* VII, 40, 1.
[45] Origen, *De Oratione* XXXI, 2.

The lifting up of the hands was so obviously connected with prayer that in the early Scriptures it can be simply synonymous with praying. The Fathers were well aware, however, that this was by no means a matter of an exclusively Christian gesture. Not only the Jews, but also the pagans, after all, lifted up their hands in prayer—prayer not necessarily directed to their idols, at that. Clement of Alexandria, for example, does not hesitate to report how the mythical Æacus, son of Zeus and a model of meekness and piety, caused a shower of rain to fall upon the arid land by lifting up his "pure hands".[46] Hence the Fathers considered it particularly important here, as in the case of other religious customs common to all mankind, to point out its specifically *Christian meaning*, even when it was a question of gestures that were already characteristic of the people of the Old Covenant.

> *Moses, the hierophant,[47] put Amalek to flight when he, imitating Christ who stretched out his hands on the Cross, held his staff sideways with both hands.[48] That is why we, too, if we stretch out our hands in prayer, will vanquish Satan. If the holy man Moses had held out his staff straight ahead and not sideways, how would his hands have become heavy then, so that he needed Aaron and Hur to hold up his hands on the right and on the left?[49]*
>
> *[Therefore] it is helpful to pray at most times [with hands spread out] in the form of a cross. For in that way we are blessed by God[50] and we also bless others. The divine Moses, too, blessed the people at the consecration of the tabernacle and at the installation of his*

[46] Clement of Alexandria, *Stromata* VII, 28, 5f.

[47] This was the name given to the "priest" of the pagan cult whose duty it was to *demonstrate* and *explain* the sacred symbols and practices. He initiated others into the religious mysteries.

[48] Ex 17:9f.

[49] Nilus of Ancyra, *Epistula* I, 86 (PG 79, 120 D). With reference to Ex 17:12.

[50] Cf. Lk 24:50.

own brother as priest, while stretching out his hands to heaven in the form of a cross.[51]

This gesture, however, was not only firmly rooted in the salvation history of the Old Covenant (even though the full depth of its meaning was revealed only in the New Covenant); the Fathers found it mysteriously prefigured even in the order of creation itself.

Indeed, all the angels pray, too. Every sort of creature prays: the cattle and the wild animals pray.[52] *They, too, bend their knee, and when they come out of their stalls or their lairs, they do not look up to heaven with an idle mouth, but rather make the breath move, each in its own way. The birds, when they come out of their nests, set out in the direction of heaven, and instead of hands they spread out their wings in the form of a cross and say something that might seem to be a prayer.*[53]

Similarly, Clement of Alexandria also saw in the direction of the axis of the oldest pagan temple a wondrous "orientation" (inadvertent on the part of the pagans themselves) of men toward the true "orient", Christ.[54]

∼

This idea of "prefiguration" and "fulfillment" is profoundly biblical, as the Gospels teach us. Paul saw in the events and personages of the Old Covenant "figures" or "types" (τύποι), the "realization" of which came only with the New Covenant.[55] In this sense the Fathers saw in Moses, who

[51] Nilus of Ancyra, *Epistula* I, 87 (PG 79, 121 A). With reference to Lev 9:22–23.

[52] Tertullian may be thinking of Ps 148.

[53] Tertullian, *De Oratione* 29.

[54] See above, pp. 69f.

[55] Cf. 1 Cor 10:6, 11.

prayed with arms outstretched in the form of a cross and
conquered Amalek in this strenuous posture, a prefigure-
ment of Christ, who conquered spiritual "Amalekites", the
demons, on the Cross. The demons, too, grasp this quite
well, and therefore they use all their machinations to force
someone who is praying to let his arms sink, as Evagrius reports about "one of the saints". "He, however, never lowered his arms until he had ended the customary prayers."[56]
Indeed, both of them knew very well what happens when
someone praying intercedes in this way in the posture of the
Crucified.

> Abba Lot went to Abba Joseph and said to him: "Abba, accord-
> ing to my strength, I recite my little office and carry out my little
> fasts, prayer, meditation, seclusion, and according to my strength
> I purify myself of my thoughts. What else must I do?" Then
> the elder stood up, spread out his hands toward heaven, and his
> fingers became like ten burning lamps. And he said to him: "If
> you will, become totally like fire!"[57]

This is the "burning prayer", as Evagrius[58] and John Cassian[59] call it, which makes man into an "angel"[60] (since an
angel consists mostly of "fire")[61] and frees him from every
earthly thing, so as to place him, like an angel, "before the
face of God".[62]

> The story was told of Abba Tithoes [that is, Sisoes] that when he
> stood in prayer, his spirit would be snatched up into the heights

---

[56] Evagrius, *De Oratione* 106, cf. 109.
[57] Joseph of Panepho 7, cf. 6.
[58] Evagrius, *De Oratione* 111.
[59] Cassian, *Conlationes* IX, 15 (Petschenig), etc.
[60] Evagrius, *De Oratione* 113.
[61] Cf. Ps 103:4.
[62] Cf. Lk 1:19.

if he did not lower his arms quickly. Now when it happened that brothers prayed with him, he hastened to lower his hands quickly, so that his spirit would not be rapt and would not linger [in the heights].[63]

~

3. *"To thee I lift up my eyes, O thou who art enthroned in the heavens"* (Ps 122:1)

The gesture of stretching out one's hands is accompanied by "lifting one's eyes" to heaven, as is already apparent from several texts. Its meaning becomes clear from the way that Scripture itself uses language. The material "heaven" or sky is only a symbol of God's "place", since in reality he is enthroned "above the heavens of the heavens".[64] The gesture is intended for God himself. The one praying directs his spiritual eyes—and hence his bodily eyes as a sign of that —"ever toward the LORD",[65] just as the eyes of servants are fixed on the hands of their master and the eyes of a maid are on the hands of her mistress,[66] so as to be of service at the slightest sign of command.

Lifting up one's eyes to heaven and fixing one's gaze on the Lord, therefore, is both a sign of intimate *familiarity* with the Lord, who is known to be present, and also a sign of willing *attention*. Hence it is recorded in many places that Christ, too, who as man prayed mightily and was the example for all Christian prayer, "raised his eyes to heaven" when he wanted to present a petition to his Father. It was

[63] Tithoes 1.
[64] Cf. Ps 56:6, 12, etc.
[65] Ps 24:15.
[66] Ps 122:2.

so at the healing of the deaf-mute,[67] at the miraculous mul-
tiplication of the loaves,[68] at the raising of Lazarus,[69] and
finally at the beginning of his farewell prayer, when Jesus
asked his Father to "glorify" him.[70]

In our Lord's case the gesture of lifting up the eyes thus
acquires a stirring solemnity; after all it is the expression of
that utterly unique relationship that exists between the Son
and his Heavenly Father. Only "in Christ" does the Christian actually dare, like him, to "lift up his eyes to heaven,"
just as "in Christ" alone he dares to say: Our Father in
heaven!

∼

Like other gestures of men of the Bible, lifting up the eyes
was carried on uninterruptedly from biblical times into the
tradition of the early Church as a lasting component of
Christian prayer. How could it have been otherwise, since
the Fathers still read Sacred Scripture from a perspective
quite different from ours!

> David says: "To thee I lift up my eyes, O thou who art enthroned
> in the heavens",[71] and: "To thee, O LORD, I lift up my soul."[72]
> For when the "eyes" of the spirit are "raised", distance themselves
> from dealing with earthly things and from permeation with all-
> too-worldly ideas, and direct themselves toward such a height that
> they look even beyond creation and strive only to contemplate God
> and to carry on a worthy and fitting conversation with him, who
> is listening: How could this not bring about the greatest benefit

[67] Mk 7:34.
[68] Mt 14:19 and parallel passages.
[69] Jn 11:4f.
[70] Jn 17:1.
[71] Ps 122:1.
[72] Ps 24:1.

*for these [souls] themselves, [who raise their] "eyes", "who with
unveiled face behold the glory of the Lord as in a mirror", and
"are changed into his likeness from glory to glory"?*[73] *For they
participate then in a certain spiritual emanation of a divine sort,
which is clear from the passage: "Let the light of thy countenance
be signed upon us, O* LORD*!"*[74]

The underlying thought is by now familiar to us: The
external gesture is only the reflection of the *interior disposition*,
which is after all the sole concern. Lifting up one's eyes to
heaven, the symbolic "place" of God, makes the body into
an "icon",[75] a representation of "the mind's upward striving into the spiritual world".[76] In fact, this is being true to
the Apostle's admonition:

*If then you have been raised with Christ, seek the things that
are above, where Christ is, seated at the right hand of God. Set
your minds on the things that are above, not on things that are
on earth. For you have died [to what is earthly], and your life is
hid with Christ in God.*[77]

Setting one's sights "on the things that are above", therefore, has the same meaning as facing east to pray: it is *turning
toward the Lord*! Just as the soul turns to the Lord in prayer,
because as a created personal being it has in the Person of
God a genuine interlocutor, so too does the human person
at prayer turn his bodily countenance, the "mirror" of the
soul, toward the Lord.

*Wherever we may be, even when we are walking along the road,
we must pray to God with our whole heart. Let us devote ourselves*

[73] 2 Cor 3:18.
[74] Origen, *De Oratione* IX, 2. Citing Ps 4:7.
[75] Ibid., XXXI, 2.
[76] Clement of Alexandria, *Stromata* VII, 40, 1.
[77] Col 3:1–3.

to prayer, with arms spread out in the form of a cross, reciting the
prayer that is recorded in the Gospel [i.e., the Our Father], and
keeping the eyes of our heart and of our body turned toward the
Lord, as it is written: "To thee I lift up my eyes, O thou who
art enthroned in the heavens! Behold, as the eyes of servants look
to the hand of their master."[78]

~

If the monk is supposed to pray everywhere as well,
"whether at gatherings for prayer . . . or in the houses, in
every place, whether in the fields or in the congregation",[79]
then standing conspicuously with arms spread out in the
form of a cross and other gestures of this sort are to be reserved, rather, for the hidden prayer in the "room".

For those who have not yet attained the true prayer of the heart,
the pain of bodily prayer comes to their assistance. By which I
mean: stretching out the hands, beating the breast, a pure look-
ing up to heaven, loud sighing, unceasing genuflections—all of
which is often not possible for us, though, because of those who
are present.[80]

Among these gestures that are not suitable in public, because they could easily arouse the curiosity of others, or at
times even their amazement, and thus become a cause of
vainglory, perhaps only "a pure looking up to heaven" is
to be excluded. For this gesture not only takes the place
of standing with hands uplifted; it is furthermore so incon-
spicuous in and of itself that the uninitiated person scarcely

---

[78] Horsiesios, *Règlements*, quoting Ps 122:1–2 (Lefort, pp. 83.8ff.);
cf. *Pachomian Koinonia*, ed. Armand Veilleux, vol. 2, CS 46 (Kalamazoo, Mich., 1981), p. 199.

[79] Ibid.

[80] John Climacus / Klimakos, *Scala Paradisi*, gr. XV, 76 (Sophronios).

understands its meaning, and our "spiritual activity" in this way remains hidden.

> *Abba Jakobos said: "I once went to Baleos to visit Abba Isidoros, the one from Nezare, and found him writing while seated in his dwelling. I remained for a while with him and observed how he often raised his eyes to heaven, without moving his lips; neither was his voice to be heard. I asked him: What are you doing, my father? He answered me: Don't you know what I am doing? Not at all, Abba, I said. Then he answered: If you do not know that, Jakobos, you have not yet been a monk for even a day! See, this is what I am saying: Jesus, have mercy on me! Jesus, help me! I praise thee, my Lord!"*[81]

~

There are moments in the life of every man, however, when he suddenly becomes painfully aware of what a privilege it actually is to raise his eyes to God—at those moments when his "face is covered with shame"[82] and he has lost his familiar boldness through a sin, an offense against God. Then, even afterward, he does not feel like standing before God and lifting up his hands to him. Rather he falls on his knees, and like the tax collector who did not even dare to "lift up his eyes to heaven", remorsefully beats his breast, that is, the place of the heart, out of which come evil thoughts,[83] and says, "O God, be merciful to me, a sinner!"[84]

Lifting up the eyes and looking toward heaven in this case would not be a sign of intimacy with God, but rather the expression of insolent *audacity*. In this sense the psalmist

[81] Eth. Coll. 13, 43; cf. Lucien Regnault, *Les Sentences des Pères du désert, nouveau recueil* (Solesmes), pp. 298–99.
[82] Ps 68:8.
[83] Mt 15:19.
[84] Lk 18:13.

speaks of "the man of haughty looks"[85] and protests, "O
LORD, my heart is not lifted up [proudly], my eyes are not
[insolently] raised too high."[86] The Fathers did not fail to
note this distinction, either. *Humility* is a regular part of their
doctrine on prayer.

> On the other hand, we recommend our petitions to God in a
> much better way when we pray with modesty and humility, with-
> out even once stretching out our hands too high, but rather merely
> lifting them up moderately and decorously, and not looking up
> too confidently either. The well-known tax collector who, when
> he prayed, showed humility and submission, not only in his pe-
> tition but also in his comportment, went away from there more
> justified than the insolent Pharisee. One's tone of voice, too, must
> be subdued; otherwise what sort of voice would be necessary if be-
> ing heard depended on how loud one could speak? God does not
> listen to voices, but to the heart, which he also scrutinizes.[87]

Likewise the master of prayer Evagrius, too, recommends
"keeping the eyes lowered during prayer"[88] and, with more
attention to the "quality" than the "quantity",[89] "praying
not pharisaically, but like the tax collector".[90]

~

But wait: the Christian, in spite of everything, must not allow himself to be robbed of that "confidence" (παῤῥησία)
that has been granted to him in Christ.[91] That is what

[85] Ps 100:5.
[86] Ps 130:1.
[87] Tertullian, *De Oratione* 17.
[88] Evagrius, *De Oratione* 110.
[89] Ibid., 151.
[90] Ibid., 102.
[91] Eph 3:12.

the tempter aims to do, however, by urging a *false humility* upon us.

> The demon, who drives the intellect to blasphemy against God and to those forbidden imaginings that I dare not even commit to writing, should not trouble us or destroy our eagerness. For the Lord is a "searcher of hearts",[92] and he knows that, while we are still in the world, we could never give ourselves over to such madness.
>
> The goal of this demon is to draw us away from prayer, so that we might no longer stand before the Lord or dare to stretch out our hands to him, against whom we had such things in mind.[93]

In this, as in similar cases, "one should not listen to them, but rather do the opposite [of what the demons are suggesting]."[94]

∽

4. *"He knelt down and prayed"* (Acts 9:40)

If standing, then, is so to speak the basic posture of those in the Bible who pray, it is still by no means the only posture. There are moments when the only appropriate posture before God is "bending the knee". Thus the man of the Bible kneels, for instance, when he *wants to beseech God for something*.[95] Peter kneels down when he asks that Dorcas, who has just died, be reawakened;[96] Paul and the elders of the congregation do the same before the Apostle's dramatic departure from Miletus,[97] and again when bidding farewell to

[92] Acts 1:24.
[93] Evagrius, *Praktikos* 46.
[94] Ibid., 22.
[95] 1 Kings 8:54.
[96] Acts 9:40.
[97] Acts 20:36.

the brothers in Tyre.[98] In the same way Paul bows his knee during his solemn intercessory prayer in Ephesians 3:14–21.

The sick,[99] or else their relatives,[100] beg Jesus for healing on their knees. But the rich man, too, who wants to follow Christ falls to his knees before him with his request.[101]

Finally, Christ himself in the Garden of Gethsemane begs his Father on his knees to allow the cup of suffering, if possible, to pass him by. Precisely what gesture is meant here and in many passages of later texts, however, is not entirely clear! For according to Luke 22:41, Christ "knelt down"; Mark 14:35 says that he "fell on the ground", whereas Matthew 26:39 says "on his face". Bending *both* knees in fact often leads to a full-length prostration on the ground. We will examine this very characteristic prayer posture in the following section.

Like standing, the bending of one knee [or both] also expresses profound *reverence*, whether it be sincere[102] or feigned, as when the Roman soldiers mocked Christ.[103] Bending the knee is a visible sign of acknowledging the majesty of the one before whom one performs this reverence.

> *To me every knee shall bow,*
> *every tongue shall swear.*
> *Only in the LORD, it shall be said of me,*
> *are righteousness and strength.*[104]

---

[98] Acts 21:5.
[99] Mk 1:40.
[100] Mt 17:14.
[101] Mk 10:17.
[102] Rom 14:11; Phil 2:10.
[103] Mt 27:29; Mk 15:19.
[104] Is 45:23f.

As was the custom for the man of the Bible, so too it was with the Fathers, for whom as a matter of course the example of the former was still the norm.

> *In saying this [that is, that one should pray while standing] we by no means intend to do away with the pious and beautiful [custom of] bending the knee! For the prophet Daniel, too, made supplication to God by getting down upon his knees at the third, sixth, and ninth hour.*[105]

Since standing to pray also expresses reverence and attentive recollection, as is fitting for a creature in an encounter with his Creator, this posture is not without dignity. Nevertheless there are moments when man forfeits this dignity and standing before God as well as lifting up the eyes would signify insolence rather than reverence. Therefore man quite spontaneously kneels on the ground before God when he wants to ask for *forgiveness of his sins.*

> *Furthermore one ought to know that, when someone accuses himself before God of his own sins and wants to beg for healing and forgiveness, kneeling is necessary; for it serves as a distinguishing mark of the one who humbles and submits himself. For Paul says: "For this reason I bow my knees before the Father, from whom every family in heaven and on earth is named."*[106]
>
> *The spiritual bending of the knee, however, so called because every existing thing humbles and lowers itself before God "in the Name of Jesus", seems to me to be indicated by the Apostle in these words: "that at the name of Jesus every knee should bow, in heaven and on earth and under the earth."*[107] *But the word of*

[105] Nilus of Ancyra, *Epistula* I, 87 (PG 79, 121 A). Referring to Dan 6:10 (11).

[106] Eph 3:14–15.

[107] Phil 2:10.

the prophet, also, "To me every knee shall bow",[108] *means the same thing.*[109]

Thus bending the knee, in the same way as standing, expresses in the body "the image of that special condition that befits the soul during prayer",[110] namely, the "humbling and abasement of the spirit", as Joseph Busnaya said.

∽

Since bending the knee is principally—but by no means exclusively—a gesture of humiliation and therefore also of *repentance*, it is understandable that it is reserved for specified times. For time, too, gains a new dimension through the fulfillment of salvation history in Christ and acquires the character of a *sign* that is directed toward this fulfillment. Only this relation to Christ makes a perhaps universally human gesture into a specifically *Christian* gesture.

Question: *If bending the knee during prayers brings those who pray closer to God than praying while standing and draws down more plentifully the divine compassion, why then do those who pray not bend the knee on the Lord's day and from Easter until Pentecost? And where did this custom in the churches originate?*

Answer: *It is because we need to be mindful at all times of both facts: both of our fall into sins and also of the grace of our Christ, through which we have risen from our fall. Therefore our bending the knee on the six days [of the week] is a symbol of our fall into sin. The fact that we do not bend the knee on the Lord's day, however, is a symbol of the Resurrection, through which we, by the grace of Christ, have been freed both from sins and also from death, which was put to death by him.*

[108] Is 45:23 / Rom 14:11.
[109] Origen, *De Oratione* XXXI, 3.
[110] Ibid., XXXI, 2.

> *This custom had its origin in apostolic times, as blessed Ire-*
> *naeus, martyr and bishop of Lyons, says in the work* On the
> Pasch,[111] *in which he also mentions the season of Pentecost, dur-*
> *ing which we do not bend the knee because it is equal to the Lord's*
> *day, for the same reason that has been given for that day.*[112]

The custom of not bending the knee on Sunday and during the entire Easter season until Pentecost is one of those
"original, unwritten traditions" of the apostles, which formerly were common to East and West but which today are
only preserved in the East.

> *According to the tradition, we must, only on this day of the Res-*
> *urrection of the Lord, refrain not only from this, but also from ev-*
> *ery attitude and practice inspired by anxiety, . . . likewise in the*
> *season of Pentecost, which we distinguish with the selfsame joy-*
> *ful conduct. Otherwise, who would hesitate to cast himself down*
> *every day before God, at least during the first prayer with which*
> *we begin the day? On fast days and station days,*[113] *however,*
> *no prayer is to be offered without bending the knee and the other*
> *attitudes of humility. For then we are not merely praying, but*
> *are also begging forgiveness and making satisfaction to God, our*
> Lord.[114]

The reasons given for the prohibition against bending the
knee at certain times may vary somewhat from one Father
to the other, but the underlying thought is always the same:

[111] Not preserved. According to the testimony of Eusebius, *Hist. Eccl.*
VI, 13, 9, Clement of Alexandria, in his own work, *On the Pasch* (which
has not been preserved either), draws from several sources, among them
Irenaeus, i.e., probably from the above-mentioned work on the same
subject.

[112] Pseudo-Justin Martyr, *Quaestiones et responsiones ad orthodoxos*,
question 115 (ΒΕΠ 4, pp. 127f.); PG 6, 1364A–1365A.

[113] That is, Wednesday and Friday.

[114] Tertullian, *De Oratione* 23.

The unity of body and soul is such that the posture of the first has to be in agreement with the interior attitude required at that particular time.

> *On the Lord's day we pray standing, [thereby] expressing the steadfast quality of the age to come. On other days, though, we bend the knee, indicating thereby the fall of the human race through sin. When we rise from bending the knee, indeed, we make clear the resurrection that has been granted to us all through Christ and which is celebrated on the Lord's day.*[115]

~

Bending the knee, as we know it now in the West, is essentially a *static* gesture. Until recently the faithful have spent a considerable amount of time during personal prayer or public devotions, even during the celebration of Holy Mass, practically immobile on their knees. To be sure, the Christians of the Eastern Church also pray occasionally on their knees, but the *bending of both knees*, which is frequently repeated many times in a row, especially when it is a matter of a penitential gesture, is most often accompanied by a short invocation much like the above-mentioned ejaculatory prayers.

This was true in the West also well into the Middle Ages. At any rate, many of the old texts do not always make it entirely clear whether they mean bending the knee in the strict sense or, instead, prostrations ("metanias"), which we will discuss in the next section. This uncertainty exists (for us), for example, in the following excerpt from a letter written by the recluse John of Gaza.

> *Therefore, if you encounter a temptation of this [nocturnal] battle [with demonic thoughts], then make seven times seven genuflec-*

---

[115] Nilus of Ancyra, *Epistula* III, 132 (PG 79, 444 D).

tions, that is, bend the knee forty-nine times, saying each time:
"Lord, I have sinned, pardon me for sake of your holy Name!" If
you are sick, however, or if it is Sunday, when it is not permitted
to make genuflections, say these words seventy times instead of
the forty-nine genuflections.[116]

It may well be that "genuflections" (γονυκλισίαι) here really means prostrations. The fact that these are two different
gestures is unambiguous, however, when we read that the
pious Countess Ada (ca. 1090) prayed the Hail Mary sixty
times a day: twenty times prostrate on the ground, twenty
times on bended knee, and twenty times standing.[117]

~

With that, we too have come to the question that perhaps
many of the readers have already asked themselves: What do
you do, then, stand or kneel? The answer is not "either-or",
but "both-and"! The various postures adopted in prayer do
not exclude each other, after all. Thus we read about a monk
who, after each psalm (which was recited standing), would
make a genuflection and then say a prayer (standing).[118] The
monks of the desert of Scetis followed much the same practice, as John Cassian tells us. After the psalmody, which was
read by lectors and which the community followed sitting,
all would get up to pray. Then they would bend the knee
and prostrate themselves on the ground to worship for a
short time, only to pray again for a longer time standing.[119]
Essentially the same "ritual" is presupposed by Benedict,

[116] Barsanuphios and John, *Epistula* 168.
[117] Cf. R. Scherschel, *Der Rosenkranz—das Jesusgebet des Westens* (Frei-
burg, 1982), p. 57.
[118] Regnault, *Série des anonymes* 1627 A.
[119] Cassian, *De Institutis* II, 7, 2 (Petschenig).

too, in his Rule.[120] A distant echo of this is still found to-day in the liturgy of Good Friday, when the deacon bids the faithful during the great intercessions: *Flectamus genua—levate*; let us bend the knee—arise.

~

5. *"Adore the* LORD *in his holy court"* (Ps 28:2)

Standing before God in prayer is an expression of that profound reverence which befits the creature in the presence of his Creator. This same interior attitude is expressed by the man of the Bible by another gesture as well: *falling down in worship* (προσκύνησις). Before the majesty of the Lord of the universe, every creature must bow down, angels[121] no less than "all kings",[122] indeed "all the earth".[123]

This "bowing down to the earth" to worship[124] is, in principle, a gesture intended only for the Person of God Almighty,[125] or else, in its derivative form, for the place in which he "dwells", the temple,[126] in the "holy courts"[127] of which the pious person falls down in worship before his "footstool".[128] Then, however, this form of reverence can also be shown to men whom God has endowed with a special spiritual authority.

[120] *Regula Benedicti*, c. 20 and 50.
[121] Ps 96:7.
[122] Ps 71:11.
[123] Ps 65:4.
[124] Gen 13:2 (Abraham before God).
[125] Deut 6:13 / Mt 4:10!
[126] Ps 5:8.
[127] Ps 28:2; 95:9.
[128] Ps 98:5, cf. 131:7.

Thus men fall down "on their face" before Christ when they become aware of the mystery of his divine being,[129] ask him for help,[130] or want to thank him for favors received.[131] The same thing happens to his apostles, who appear and act in his power and with his authority.[132]

Later, in the ancient monastic literature, there is very frequent mention of one monk falling down before another, "making a metania", as it is called. Here, however, this gesture of the most profound humility has a very particular meaning: It underscores the *plea for forgiveness*. Hence also the term "metania" (μετάνοια)—remorse, penance, conversion, which is consistently used in this connection. The only true monk is the one who is ready to humiliate himself in this way even before someone who has done *him* an injustice. From this we can understand how one Father can go so far as to maintain that it was Satan who caused Adam to hide himself after the Fall in Paradise, so that he would not make a metania when he met God and thus be forgiven.[133]

∿

As a prayer gesture, the "metania" (*prostratio*) has constantly been a part of the spiritual life since biblical times, both in the East and also—for over a millennium—in the West.

A brother asked an elder: "Is it good to make many metanias?" The elder said: "We see that God appeared to Joshua, the son of Nun, while he was lying on his face."[134]

---

[129] Mt 8:2; 9:18, etc.
[130] Lk 5:12.
[131] Lk 17:16.
[132] Acts 10:25.
[133] Regnault, *Série des anonymes* 1765.
[134] Nau 301. Referring to Josh 7:6, 10.

As we see, the one praying throws himself down *full length on the ground*. "He throws himself down on his face and prays to God",[135] just as Christ did in the Garden of Gethsemane.[136] This gesture is also listed among the "Nine Ways of Prayer of Saint Dominic" and was retained well into modern times among the Dominicans in the form of the *venia*, an expression of humbling oneself before a confrère. Within the Eastern Church two different forms of the prostration developed at an early date.

> *The order of the prostrations is as follows: One should fall down before the cross until the knees and the head [that is, actually the forehead] touch the ground.*
>
> *In bowing, though, the knees do not reach the ground, but only the hands and the head, while the body remains suspended in the air.*[137]

Corresponding to this distinction even today in that part of the East that is influenced by Byzantium are the "great metania", in which the knees, hands, and forehead touch the ground, and the "little metania", the *profunda* of the Latin monks, in which only the right hand touches the ground. There is no prayer, whether said in a congregation or in private, that is not accompanied even today in the Christian East by numerous "metanias". What, in fact, would a prayer be without metanias? It would remain "routine, cold, and shallow" (Joseph Busnaya).

Of course, what was said earlier about genuflections is naturally true for metanias as well: Every week on the Lord's day and during the entire Pentecost season, the great metanias are forbidden, because they are penitential gestures.

---

[135] Johannes Kolobos 40.
[136] Mt 26:39; however, see above, p. 163.
[137] Joseph Busnaya, in Chabot, "Vie", p. 397.

∽

If Adam would have been forgiven had he only made a metania in all humility before God after his Fall, then it is clear
that this gesture is a mighty weapon against the attacks of
the evil one. Thus an elder advises a brother who is sorely
tempted:

> Stand up, pray and make a metania, while saying: "Son of God,
> have mercy on me!"[138]

Yet not only during private prayer, but also in services
of public worship, the Fathers made a certain number of
metanias.

> The above-mentioned prayers begin and end [among the Egyptian
> Desert Fathers] as follows: As soon as a psalm is finished, they
> do not bend the knee hastily, as do some of us in this area who,
> even before the psalm is actually finished, throw ourselves down
> quickly to pray, so as to get to the end of it as quickly as possible.
> Since we want to surpass the measure [of twelve psalms] that was
> determined from time immemorial by the Fathers, we also rush to
> the end, reckoning how many psalms still remain, thinking more
> of refreshing our tired bodies than of the benefits and advantages
> of prayer![139]

∽

For centuries the gesture of prayer called the metania, which
John Cassian describes here for his Western readers, was no
less familiar in the West than in the East. The *Regula Magistri*[140] assumes knowledge of it no less than the Rule of
Saint Benedict.[141] Not only monks, but also the Christian

---

[138] Nau 184.
[139] Cassian, *De Institutis* II, 7, 1 (Petschenig).
[140] *Regula Magistri*, c. 48, 10–11 (de Vogüé).
[141] *Regula Benedicti*, c. 20, 4–5.

faithful made prostrations during their private prayers. In the eleventh century the pious Countess Ada, as we have seen, made twenty prostrations daily, while the holy hermit Aybert (d. 1140) threw himself down onto the ground fifty times.[142] A young monk of the desert made as many as one hundred metanias "according to the custom".[143] Here again we are faced with the question of the proper *measure*, which arises with all gestures that are repeated often. How many "prayers" should one recite, how many genuflections should one make, how many metanias?

> *As for the number of genuflections[144] that we have to make during the five weekdays in the course of a day and a night, we know that our godly fathers set it at three hundred. For on every Saturday and on every Sunday, and also on several other days and weeks that have been determined by tradition for certain mysterious and unpublished reasons, it is commanded that we refrain from these genuflections. There are those who surpass this number, others fall short of it, each one according to his strength or his free decision. You too, then, do what you can! Blessed, nevertheless, is he who at all times does violence to himself in everything that pertains to God. For "the kingdom of heaven has suffered violence, and men of violence take it by force."[145]*

Kallistos and Ignatios are writing for "hesychasts", monks who live in complete seclusion and dedicate themselves entirely to prayer. Each one must ascertain the proper measure with his spiritual father, who is able to weigh in the balance the factors of age, health and constitution, and, most importantly, spiritual maturity. In the spiritual life a "rule" is never

---

[142] Scherschel, *Rosenkranz*, pp. 57–58.

[143] Regnault, *Série des anonymes* 1741.

[144] Meant here are *metanias*.

[145] Kallistos and Ignatios Xanthopuloi, *Precise Methods*, c. 39 (*Philokalia*, vol. 4 [Athens, 1961], p. 239). Quoting Mt 11:12.

a rigid law or an unchangeable obligation. It is a *guideline* for things that a man has *voluntarily* set out to do, for the glory of God and the healing of his soul.

~

Today this practice, which in former times was the common property of all Christendom, has almost completely disappeared in the West. Most of the sons of Benedict, whose Rule does foresee prostrations during prayer, are probably barely acquainted with it from their own experience. The lay faithful, at any rate, will have experienced it as a liturgical rite during the Good Friday liturgy. Both groups, as a result, have been robbed of a mighty weapon in the spiritual life.

Isaac of Nineveh teaches what sort of power is inherent in metanias. It is a question of those debilitating periods of total *interior darkness*, all too familiar to modern man as well, when one is incapable of saying even the slightest prayer. On those occasions, Isaac recommends taking refuge in repeated metanias, even if it is apparently without feeling and one seems to remain completely cold inside. For nothing frightens the adversary more than this gesture of profound obeisance, and hence he will employ all his machinations to keep us from making it[146]—as he once kept Adam in Paradise from casting himself down to worship God after his Fall.

We have already encountered this underlying notion that the demons observe very attentively what we do and say. Even when we ourselves are distracted and are not at all aware of the meaning of the words in the psalms, the demons

[146] Isaac of Nineveh, c. 49 (Amsterdam: Wensinck, 1923), pp. 228ff. Cf. Holy Transfiguration Monastery, *The Ascetical Homilies of Saint Isaac the Syrian* (Boston, 1984), pp. 387f.

still hear them and tremble, as it is written![147] Why this is
so is explained in a passage by Evagrius.

> *"They watch my steps": In order to learn by observing what we
> do. For the demons are by no means "knowers of the heart".*[148]
> Only *"he who fashions the hearts of them all" can know [them]
> as well. Therefore God alone is rightly called the one who "knows
> the hearts [of all men]".*[149]

The demon is and remains the "stranger", who has only
indirect access to our "heart", the center of our person. He
knows from experience, that is, from keen observation, that
this "heart", from which indeed all "evil thoughts" originate,[150] betrays itself through "body language" of which we
are most often completely unaware. Sounding quite modern, Evagrius states that the demons draw inferences about
the condition of our heart from our gestures, our expressions, the tone of our voice, in short from the totality of
our external behavior, and then they adapt their tactics accordingly.[151]

We ought to take advantage of this union of body and soul
and benefit from it during prayer, as well! And we should
do this, not only in view of the demons that prowl about us,
but also and primarily to confront the resistance of our own
halting, faithless heart. Repeating the metania gesture, even
when it is performed only with the body, is just as effective
as tears in breaking the spell of that interior "wildness" and
insensitivity that seems to kill all spiritual life within us. In
a mysterious way the body, which in its posture is actually

---

[147] Barsanuphios and John, *Epistula* 711, see above pp. 128f.
[148] Evagrius, *In Ps.* 55:7 δ.
[149] Evagrius, *In Ps.* 32:15 ι; Acts 1:24.
[150] Mt 15:19.
[151] Evagrius, *Epistula* 16; *In Prov.* 6:13 (Géhin 76).

the "icon" of the soul's interior disposition (Origen), ultimately draws the reluctant soul along with it.

∼

6. ". . . let him take up his cross daily" (Lk 9:23)

One of the most ancient, exclusively Christian gestures, which in any case is not restricted to the time of prayer, is making the sign of the cross, or, to use the precise term, "sealing" or "signing" oneself [with the sign of the cross].

> At every step of the way, when going in and going out, when putting on our clothes and shoes, while washing, eating, lighting lamps, going to sleep, while sitting down, and in whatever action we are carrying out, we imprint on our forehead the little sign [of the cross].[152]

Origen testifies for the Greek-speaking regions in the Orient that "all the faithful, before they begin any sort of activity, especially before prayer or before *lectio divina* [devotional reading from Scripture]" mark their forehead with the sign of the cross. They did this, because they saw in the letter *tau* (written in Old Hebrew as a cross (+) and in Greek as a "T"), which according to Ezekiel 9:4 was marked on the foreheads of those who were faithful, "a prophecy of the customary sign [of the cross] on the foreheads of Christians".[153] This was probably intended by the seer of the Apocalypse when he spoke of "seal[ing] the servants of our God upon their foreheads".[154] Luke 9:23, too, could have originally been meant in the sense of such a distinctive "marking".

---

[152] Tertullian, *De Corona* 3 (Kroymann).
[153] Origen, *Selecta in Ez 9* (PG 13, 800/801).
[154] Rev 7:3, etc.

~

However historians may explain the origin of this gesture, for the Fathers it was a question of one of those "original, unwritten traditions"[155] that go back to the apostles and thus to the early Church herself, even though they—intentionally—were not set down in writing definitively.[156] Tertullian also refers to this tradition of the Church in the work cited above, which he wrote in the year 211. A text that originated in the circle of Pachomian monks in Egypt makes clear that this gesture, too—just like facing the east while praying—always reminded the early Christians of their *baptism*, that is, of the all-surpassing event to which they owed their Christianity and hence their salvation.

> *Let us sign ourselves as we begin our prayers with the sign of baptism, let us make upon our forehead the sign of the cross, as on that day when we were baptized, and as it is written in the prophet Ezekiel.*[157] *Let us not raise our hand only as far as the mouth or the beard, but rather let us bring it to our forehead, while saying in our heart: "We have signed ourselves with the seal!" While this is not of the same nobility as the seal of baptism, nevertheless on the day when we were baptized, the sign of the cross was imprinted on the forehead of each one of us.*[158]

~

This gesture of signing oneself with the cross, like no other gesture, identifies the Christian as a "Christian", as a man whose salvation comes solely from Christ's *death on the*

---

[155] Evagrius, *Mal. cog.* 33, 28 (Géhin-Guillaumont; PG 40, 1240 D).
[156] Basil the Great, *De Spiritu Sancto* XXVII, 66 (Pruche).
[157] Ezek 9:4.
[158] Horsiesios, *Règlements* (Lefort, pp. 83, 16ff.; cf. *Pachomian Koinonia*, 2:199).

Cross, into which he has been drawn in a mysterious manner through the sacrament of baptism.

> *"To bear the sign of the cross"*,[159] *though, means "to carry death around with me"*,[160] *by "renouncing all"*[161] *even in this life, since there is a difference between the love of what the flesh has begotten and the love of what the soul has accomplished for the sake of knowledge.*[162]

For this reason the holy sign of the cross, which we make over ourselves or others, is always a profession of faith in the *victory* that Christ on the Cross won against every hostile power. For the Fathers always made use of this sign, also, whenever they knew that they were confronted with these hostile powers. Indeed, Anthony the Great taught his disciples that the demons and their phantasms were in reality "nothing and quickly disappear, especially when a person arms himself with faith and the sign of the cross".[163] The same is true of all forms of *pagan magic.*[164]

> *If you often seal your own forehead and your heart with the sign of our Lord's Cross, the demons will take flight from you trembling, for they shudder vehemently at this blessed sign!*[165]
>   *If you want to wipe out the bad memories left in the mind and the multifarious attacks of the enemy, then arm yourself speedily with the recollection of our Savior and with the ardent invocation of his exalted name by day and by night, while sealing yourself*

---

[159] Cf. Lk 14:27. Clement spontaneously replaces the word "cross" here with "sign" (σημεῖον), because he understands the text to refer to the *sign of the cross.* Cf. also Mt 24:30, the "sign of the Son of Man".
[160] Cf. 2 Cor 4:10.
[161] Cf. Lk 14:33.
[162] Clement of Alexandria, *Stromata* VII, 79, 7.
[163] Athanasius, *Vita Antonii*, c. 23, 4 (Bartelink), cf. 13, 5.
[164] Ibid., c. 78, 5.
[165] Nilus of Ancyra, *Epistula* II, 304 (PG 79, 349 C).

*often, both on the forehead and on the breast, with the sign of our
Lord's Cross. For as often as the name of our Savior Jesus Christ
is pronounced and the seal of the Lord's Cross is placed on the
heart and the forehead and on the other members [of the body],
the power of the enemy is indubitably quelled, and the wicked
demons flee trembling from us.*[166]

As great as the power of the sign of the cross is, it is not a
question of a magical gesture. It is *faith* that makes it mighty!

*When you are tempted, sign your forehead with devotion. This
sign of the Passion is shown against the devil, when anyone makes
it in faith, and not in order to be pleasing to men but presenting
it deliberately like a shield; the adversary will see the strength of
spirit that comes from the heart.*[167]

~

The sign of the cross was probably made at first "in the name
of our Savior Jesus Christ" and then later "in the name of
the Father and of the Son and of the Holy Spirit".[168] Because there is such power in this holy sign, it goes without
saying that it must not be used out of mere vainglory, nor
for that matter thoughtlessly. For this reason the tradition of
the Church has determined the manner in which we should
cross ourselves.

The texts from the patristic era that have been cited
thus far teach that the "little sign" (*signaculum*) at first was
traced mainly on one's own forehead, probably with just one

[166] Ibid., III, 278 (PG 79, 521 B/C).

[167] Hippolytus of Rome, *Traditio Apostolica* 42 (B. Botte, *La Tradition apostolique de Saint Hippolyte: Essai de reconstitution*, Liturgiewissenschaftliche Quellen und Forschungen, 39 [Münster, 1963], p.
64; English translation from the German of W. Geerlings, *Fontes
Christiani* I [Freiburg, 1991], p. 309).

[168] Barsanuphios and John, *Epistula* 46.

finger, both in the Greek East and in the Latin West. In the same way, then, one also "sealed" the lips, the heart, and so on, on certain occasions, until eventually this developed into that great gesture familiar to us all, through which the believer places himself with his entire body, so to speak, under the Cross of Christ.

> *Furthermore one must marvel at how the demons and many sorts of sickness are driven away by the sign of the precious and life-giving Cross, which anyone can make without cost or difficulty. And who can number the panegyrics composed in its honor? The holy Fathers, though, have handed down to us the meaning of this holy sign [of the cross] in order to refute heretics and unbelievers.*
>
> *The two fingers and the one hand, then, represent the crucified Lord Jesus Christ, whom we profess as having two natures in one Person. The right hand recalls his unlimited might[169] and his sitting at the right hand of the Father.[170] And one begins [to trace] it from above because of his descent from the heavens to us.[171] Furthermore [the movement of the hand] from the right side to the left drives away the enemies and indicates that the Lord through his invincible might has conquered the devil, who is on the left, a powerless and gloomy being.[172]*

It is easy to see that this "two-finger cross", which is well known to us as a *gesture of blessing* from countless ancient depictions of Christ in the East and the West, and which the Russian "Old Believers" have preserved to this day, must have arisen in a milieu where there were "unbelievers" and "heretics". The *two* fingers and the *one* hand are—in oppo-

---

[169] Ps 117:15, etc.

[170] Ps 109:1 / Mt 22:44, etc.

[171] Eph 4:10.

[172] Peter Damascene, Book I, *On the Differences between Thoughts and Provocations* (*Philokalia*, vol. 3, [Athens, 1960], p. 110). Referring at the conclusion to Mt 25:33f., etc.

sition to the Monophysites and Nestorians—a mute profession of the *two* natures of the incarnate Word in one "hypostasis" or Person. Much older and not limited to any time or place, in contrast, is the biblical symbolism of "above—below", "right—left", which even today is deeply rooted in everyday language and customs.

As the above-mentioned christological disputes died down and a context that was free of polemics emerged, the sign of the cross then revealed the whole wealth of its symbolism and took on its definitive form.

> One should make the sign of the cross with [the first] three fingers [of the right hand], because it is traced while invoking the Trinity —of which the prophet says: "Who has poised [that is, weighed] with three fingers the bulk of the earth?"[173]—in such a way that one goes down from high to low and then from right to left, because Christ descended from heaven to earth and passed over from the Jews to the Gentiles.[174]

The way of making the sign of the cross that Pope Innocent III described, while still a deacon of the Church in Rome, was customary at that time also in the territories of the Eastern Church, and Orthodox Christians still make it that way today. Even after the Great Schism of 1054, then, the sign of the Holy Cross, a gesture with profound, carefully thought out symbolism, continued for the time being to unite East and West.

As the following lines of the chapter just quoted make clear, however, at that time "some people" already were beginning to trace the horizontal beam of the cross in the opposite direction, that is, from left to right, as is the

[173] Is 40:12 (Vulgate).
[174] Innocent III, *De Sacro Altaris Mysterio*, lib. II, c. XLV (PL 217, 825).

practice today only in the West. Symbolic and practical reasons for this were cited. As the explanation went, we must pass from misery (symbolized by the left, "bad" side) to glory (symbolized by the "good" right side), just as Christ himself passed from death to life and from the nether world to Paradise. Furthermore, one ought to cross oneself in the very same way in which one is signed with the cross during a blessing.

Innocent offers no comment on the symbolic reason, but he does not grant the validity of the practical one. He correctly points out that we do not make the sign of the cross over others as though they had their backs turned to us, but rather face to face! Therefore the priest traces the horizontal beam from left to right, so that the believer may receive it from right to left, just as he crosses himself.

It is regrettable that "some people" soon became "many" and then "all", despite the very clear words of this great Pope, and that we thus lost one more bit of that common heritage that formerly united East and West. It is even more regrettable that today in the West there is probably next to no one left who still knows the sacred symbolism of the sign of the cross, as the Fathers handed it down to us.

CONCLUSION

The "treasure in earthen vessels"

(2 Cor 4:7)

"The faith is evaporating"—we took this lament as the point of departure for our study. It is evaporating, we answered, because it is not "practiced". This can be seen as plain as day in the present state of personal prayer and its "practices". After all, from time immemorial prayer has been, so to speak, a barometer for the intensity of faith.

The traditions of the Church, of Scripture, and of the Fathers have left us an abundant treasure, not only of texts, but also of customs, forms, gestures, and so on, associated with prayer. In the modern age—especially in Western Christianity—little or almost nothing of it remains. Where these seemingly "external" things are lacking, however, prayer becomes "routine, cold, and shallow" (Joseph Busnaya), and faith itself, which ought to be expressed in it, imperceptibly grows cold as well and finally evaporates.

∼

The early Fathers were well aware that these things, which in their view were by no means mere "externals", are always in danger of being neglected and ultimately forgotten, once their meaning is no longer understood. Early on, therefore, Tertullian in the Latin West and Origen in the Greek East considered it appropriate to follow up their treatises *On*

Prayer with a "practical" appendix, in which this "original",
that is, apostolic, albeit "unwritten tradition" (Makarios of
Alexandria, cited by Evagrius) of the Church would again
be called to mind.

On the other hand, many people today conclude from
the—apparent—extinction of these traditions that there is
no returning to the past! The healing of the spiritual crisis
in the West lies "ahead of us" rather than "behind us", they
say. The present task, indeed, in a spirit of a broad-based
ecumenism, is to learn from the great religions of humanity
and to borrow from them the things with which we have
been losing touch. Consequently, for many people, adopt-
ing various "methods"—of meditation, for instance—from
other religions has become a matter of course that they do
not even question. This seems possible, quite simple in fact,
because, as they say, "Zen is not a belief system but a discipline" (R. Resch), which therefore can be detached from its
Buddhist setting with no problem whatsoever. Zen, indeed,
has become for many *the* "way" upon which they hope to
reach an authentic "experience of God".

Sine ira et studio let us pose a few questions here at the
conclusion and attempt to give the kind of answers that the
Fathers recommend. This will be useful with respect to our
main subject as well.

∼

As the above-cited statement by a Western Zen-master illus-
trates, "praxis" (or "discipline") and "faith" are regarded
by many as two dimensions standing *independently*, one beside the other, which therefore can also be separated from
each other without any problem. Very few Christians who
practice Zen, after all, have in mind a formal conversion to
Buddhism. But does this mental distinction have any basis

whatsoever in reality? Let us hear again what Evagrius has to say.

In the prologue to his treatise *On Prayer*, Evagrius praises that anonymous friend who asked him to compose it for demanding not only those chapters that owe their existence to ink and paper, but also those that have their basis in the intellect through love and avoiding all thought of evil, which virtues are the fruit of the "practical" life.[1] Evagrius then continues:

> *Well, then! Since "all things are twofold, one opposite the other," according to [the saying of] the wise man Jesus [Sirach],[2] accept [these chapters] according to the letter and the spirit, and understand that the meaning absolutely precedes the letter. For if this did not exist, the letter would not either.*

In what follows, Evagrius applies this distinction to prayer. Prayer, too, consists of a twofold manner; the one is "practical", the other "contemplative". They are related to each other as "quantity" is to "quality" or, in biblical terms, as "the letter" is to the "spirit" (πνεῦμα)[3] or to the meaning (νοῦς).

The "practical manner" of prayer—which also includes everything we call "method"—does not exist at all as something separate in and of itself. It is nothing more than the *form assumed* by the "contemplative manner", without which those "letters" would have neither "spirit" nor "meaning" and, in fact, would not even exist. Accordingly one cannot separate the "practical manner" from its "meaning" and try to practice it for its own sake, either in Christianity or in any other religion you may choose.

[1] Evagrius, *Praktikos* 81.
[2] Sir 42:25.
[3] Cf. 2 Cor 3:6.

It is likely that all the Fathers thought as Evagrius did. Origen, for instance, for whom the gestures characteristic of Christian prayer are "so to speak the image of the special condition of the soul" during "prayer [offered] . . . in the body", recommends that one should "stretch out one's soul, so to speak, before stretching out one's hands, and lift up one's spirit to God before lifting up one's eyes, and, before standing at one's place to pray, [one should] raise one's mind from the earth and place it in the presence of the Lord of all."[4]

~

Continuing this train of thought, we may conclude that "spirit" and "meaning" always precede the "letter", and not only conceptually; on the contrary, the "practical manner" of prayer owes its concrete *form* to the "contemplative manner", that is, to the contents of the Christian faith. This means, though, that the "practical manner" has no other purpose than to provide the "spirit" of the "contemplative manner" with precisely those *means* that it requires in order to become a reality in the person who prays.

The "twofold, spiritual and bodily worship" (John Damascene) that we offer to God is therefore a self-contained *unity*. The "contemplative manner" and the "practical manner" of prayer mutually affect one another, each in its own way. A "practical manner" or a "method" without an intrinsic "spirit" informing it is *meaningless*. Conversely, however, the "contemplative manner" would remain *insubstantial* if it failed to take on a form within the praying person (who consists of soul *and* body) as a "praxis" that was appropriate and directed toward it.

[4] Origen, *De Oratione* XXXI, 2.

By "method", in the sense in which Evagrius uses the term, is not meant any mere "technique". The "practices" that have been the main subject of this book are rather the sensual-perceptible side of that "spiritual method" which "purifies the passionate part of the soul" and which Evagrius[5] calls *praktike*—specifically, in the case of the prayer life, the "practical manner of prayer". Evagrius alludes to this comprehensive "spiritual method" when he speaks of those "chapters about prayer", which do not owe their existence to ink and paper, but rather "take their place in the intellect through love and avoiding all thought of evil", as the fruit of the *cooperation* of "divine grace and human effort".[6]

> *Love is the daughter of dispassion,*
> *while dispassion is the flower of the* praktike.
> Praktike, *in turn, is based upon keeping the commandments.*
> *Their guardian, though, is the fear of God,*
> *which is an offshoot of right faith.*
> *Faith, now, is an immanent good, which is naturally found*
> *even in those who do not yet believe in God.*[7]

Although the *capacity* to believe is an immanent good (even in the person who *presently* does not yet believe), thanks to the creation of *all* men "in the image of God", it still requires *God's self-revelation* in order to awaken that "right faith in the adorable and Holy Trinity".[8] Only this right faith can lead the "practical" believer by stages to that "perfect and spiritual love in which the prayer in spirit and in truth becomes real".[9]

[5] Evagrius, *Praktikos* 78.
[6] Evagrius, *In Ps. 17:21* ιβ.
[7] Evagrius, *Praktikos* 81.
[8] Evagrius, *In Ps. 147:2* α.
[9] Evagrius, *De Oratione* 77.

From what has been said we must conclude that, in any case, a so-called "neutral praxis", which each one could arbitrarily fill up with "meaning" and which would lead all men, believers and nonbelievers, to the same goal, in the opinion of our Fathers in faith, does not exist and in principle cannot exist.

For our subject in particular it follows that those "practices" that were discussed on the preceding pages constitute the *formation* of biblical-Christian prayer, as this process was realized in the course of salvation history. They are in no way "time-bound externals", but rather the "earthen vessels" in which the imperishable "treasure" has come down to us. Although the apostles intentionally did not set them down permanently in writing, the Fathers, for instance, Basil the Great, but even earlier Tertullian, rightly ascribe to these practices the same authority as he ascribes to the traditions that were set down in writing.

The Fathers at any rate were already well aware—Origen mentions it—that among the customs of the Church there are many that indeed "must be followed by all, without all of them [necessarily] knowing the reasons for them."[10] This widespread *ignorance* means that these customs run the risk of being disparaged and ultimately neglected and abandoned. For this reason, as we have said, the Fathers soon recognized the necessity of explaining the sense of these ecclesiastical customs, so that the disparagement of these unwritten apostolic traditions would not "unintentionally [cause] damage to be done to the Gospel itself in important passages."[11] Every generation faces this necessity anew, and it is the duty of the teachers of the Church not only to preserve in an

---

[10] Origen, *Num. hom.* V, 1 (Baehrens).
[11] Basil, *De Spiritu Sancto* XXVII, 66, 8f. (Pruche).

unadulterated form both the "written" and the "unwritten tradition", but also to proclaim them anew to the faithful at all times. And if that does not happen. . . ?

~

The "practical manner of prayer", Evagrius said—and this is true for the *praktike* in general—can be compared to "the letter" (or "writing" or "the text", since the Greek word γράμμα can mean all of these) that owes its existence to the preexisting "meaning", to which it in turn gives expression, thus making it communicable. In other words, all of those "practical" elements of the spiritual life (we have presented a few of them here) together constitute, as it were, a "language" that makes the "spirit" of prayer accessible to someone who prays. Only the person who has a command of this "language" is capable of conveying to others as well the hidden "meaning" of prayer.

Therefore the loss of this "language" unquestionably leads to a sort of *speechlessness*, that is, the inability to communicate to others that "meaning" which we ourselves no longer have experienced existentially. Today this is called a "break in the tradition": the inability to understand the "language" of our Fathers in faith, and our mute helplessness before our own children.

~

Nevertheless, nature abhors a vacuum. The parents might be content to have lost the "way", but their children will not be reconciled so easily to the idea. They search for new "ways", unaware that they thereby "introduce things that are foreign to our path", thus exposing themselves to the danger of becoming, themselves, "strangers to the ways of our Savior" (Evagrius).

The fact is, whether you like it or not, that the choice of the "means" already determines the result. *Ce que tu fais, te fait,* as it is put succinctly in French: *What you do, makes you!* Anyone who devotes himself to "practices" and "methods" that are not home-grown in the soil of his own faith will imperceptibly be led toward that "faith" which developed these practices as a genuine expression of itself. Today plenty of people are going through this painful experience, even though many do not dare admit even to themselves that they have strayed from the path.

~

What is to be done, then, when someone realizes that he is uprooted? Well, to use the biblical expression, he must "convert" to "what was from the beginning"! When a person has "abandoned the love [he] had at first", he must "remember then from what [he has] fallen, repent, and do the works [he] did at first".[12] In the spiritual life—and not only there—this means that one "asks about the paths of those who went ahead of us in the right way", so as "to follow in their footsteps". One must "converse with them", which in most cases means: study their lives and their writings, in order to "learn of them". Then, having "heard [from them] what is helpful", it is a matter of beginning "at the lowest place", with those "externals" that were discussed here, and "demanding of oneself also the accomplishment of the same deeds of the Fathers amid great labors". Only the person who undertakes these labors can hope to be deemed worthy one day of that same knowledge of God that we admire so much in the holy Fathers.

[12] Rev 2:4–5.

~

Nevertheless, it cannot be proved conclusively that all of this really is the case, just as it is presented here. To quote Evagrius Ponticus one last time: For those who content themselves either with "speaking with pleasure about the deeds of the Fathers" or merely studying them "academically", no matter how great or sincere their interest may be, it is inevitable that "much [will remain] hidden, other things [will be] obscure", and at any rate they will miss what is essential.

For those who set foot on the same path [which the feet of the holy Fathers have marked out], nevertheless, these things will be clear. [13]

~

---

[13] Evagrius, *Praktikos*, prol. [9].

APPENDIX

Practical Advice

The *Catechism of the Catholic Church*, in part 4 about "Christian Prayer", includes a short reference to the "favorable place for prayer", which says:

> For personal prayer, this can be a "prayer corner" with the Sacred Scriptures and icons, in order to be there, in secret, before our Father.[1]

Therefore it might be useful, based on the tradition of the holy Fathers set forth in this little book, to draw a few practical conclusions for setting up such a "prayer corner" and for the little office of prayers that the Christian could carry out there, "in secret", before his Heavenly Father. For the most beautiful thoughts about prayer remain fruitless, after all, if they do not lead *to prayer itself*.

1. *The choice of the right place and setting it up*

So as to be able to have a personal "conversation" with the Father "in secret", the "prayer corner" should be as *secluded* and *peaceful* as the "room" behind "closed doors" of which Christ spoke.

It goes without saying that it should be set up to face *toward the east*. After all, the person praying is turning toward

[1] § 2691.

the "true light",[2] God, who "has called us out of darkness into his marvelous light."[3]

Therefore the corner should not be without a *light*, in the form of an icon lamp and/or candles. Lighting this lamp [or these candles] before dawn and at nightfall is part of that "spiritual worship"[4] which the person praying performs before God in secret.

The *orientation* of the prayer corner toward the east is best indicated with a *cross*, as has been the custom from time immemorial. In selecting such a cross, care should be taken that it depicts not only the suffering and death of the Son of Man (a crucifix) but also his victory over death. Many old (and modern) crosses very beautifully combine *the Tree of Life* and *the wood of the Cross* into one image and thus pictorially remind the person praying that he does so while facing Paradise, his "original home".

On the right and the left of this "sign of the Lord", or else beneath it, one can hang *icons* of Christ (to the right) and the Mother of God (to the left), as well as favorite saints. They make present in picture form our Savior and those in whom "God has shown himself wonderful [LXX]",[5] and help the person praying alone to realize that he always prays "in the communion of saints".

On a *prie-dieu* or prayer stand the "instruments" of daily prayer should be available: the Sacred Scriptures, the Psalter, or other prayer books that one might need, a rosary. . .

A little oratory of this kind, though it may remain hidden from the eyes of men, is what turns the dwelling of any Christian into a "domestic church"! Like a pinch of salt,

[2] 1 Jn 2:8.
[3] 1 Pet 2:9.
[4] Rom 12:1.
[5] Ps 67:36.

which seems to disappear in the "world", it actually flavors and seasons it.

~

2. *The times for prayer*

The daily routine of the man of ancient times, divided as it was into large periods of three hours each, followed a rhythm that was much more peaceful than that of modern man, who is ruled by the dictates of the precision clock. The choice of favorable times for prayer is therefore that much more important.

Like the man of the Bible, the early monastic Fathers preferred to pray their two "offices" during the time *after sunset* and *before sunrise*. These are the moments that even a modern man—with a certain amount of self-discipline—can most readily reserve for prayer. Someone who offers to God the beginning of the day or of the night as "first fruits" can hope that the rest of the day or night, too, will be *sanctified*. It will also be easier for him to keep the "memory of God" alive in his heart in the midst of all his activities.

However extensive or brief one's daily prayer may be, the most important thing is its *regularity*, that of "persevering in prayer".[6]

3. *The "little office"*

The Church's Liturgy of the Hours—in the East to a much greater extent than in the West—became more and more differentiated and also more voluminous in the course of the centuries. The "breviary" represents an early attempt to reduce this Liturgy of the Hours to a more compact form.

---

[6] Acts 2:42.

The liturgical reforms of the last centuries have led to further abridgements in the Western Church.

Many Christians (clergy and religious among them) are convinced that praying long offices is something "typically monastic". The early Desert Fathers, even though they had withdrawn from all worldly affairs and lived entirely for prayer, nonetheless always speak about their "little office" (μικρὰ συναξις). In fact both of their offices, each with twelve psalms and the corresponding prayers, were not particularly long. The numerous "prayers", too, that they said by day during their work did not go beyond the length of an Our Father, to say nothing at all about the short ejaculatory prayers, which comprised only a few words.

Anyone who would like to follow in the footsteps of the holy Fathers and enter the "place of prayer", anyone who yearns for the "state of prayer", would therefore do well to devise for himself an office suited to his capabilities, which will *awaken in him and maintain the spirit of prayer*. The goal, indeed, is to keep "the mind in prayer all day long".

For personal prayer, the most suitable book is the *Psalter*, which should be arranged accordingly for this purpose. This means dividing the long psalms into smaller sections, with "quality" rather than "quantity" in mind.

> *Therefore [the holy Fathers] consider it more useful to sing ten verses with understanding and attention than to rattle off an entire psalm in a disorderly way.*[7]

In keeping with this wise rule, each person should undertake to pray the number of psalms that corresponds to his abilities. Someone who would like to preserve the hallowed number of *twelve* psalms for the morning and evening

---

[7] Cassian, *De Institutis* II, 11, 2 (Petschenig).

office with the prayers that follow them can easily do so by subdividing the Psalter accordingly.

In principle, the psalms should be read *in sequence*, without picking and choosing and above all without leaving any out; it is, after all, primarily a question of hearing the Word of God.

As one wishes, anyone can enrich this psalmody with hymns from the Church's tradition or round it off with Scripture readings.

Instead of this relatively free-form office, many perhaps will prefer the *Church's Liturgy of the Hours* as a set framework. In that case, though, it should be noted that this really presupposes a praying *community* with various readers, singers, and so forth.

In any case, one should take care that the "little office" never degenerates into a mere formality, a duty that is discharged conscientiously but without interior involvement. The freedom that many experienced masters of the spiritual life concede to the person who prays regularly[8] is meant precisely to cut off any sort of formalism at the roots and to lead to "true prayer". As experience has shown, the alternation of psalm and prayer is a good guideline.

The *prayer of the heart*, in and of itself, is not bound to any particular prayer time, being as it is the "breathing of the soul". Experience teaches, though, that it is helpful to devote a particular period of the morning and evening office to it as well, because in that way it more easily becomes a part of one's flesh and blood.

Since apostolic times the believer has prayed the *Our Father three times a day* (*Didache*). It is *the* prayer of the Chris-

---

[8] One may read, for example, Isaac of Nineveh, c. 80 (Wensinck, pp. 366ff.); cf. *The Ascetical Homilies* (Boston, 1984), pp. 365–75.

tian, which the Lord himself taught. Therefore it goes without saying that one should pray the Our Father often during
the day—never repeating it mindlessly, however. It should
always be the high point of each prayer time, and its special
character should also find expression in the posture assumed
by the person praying it.

4. *Methods and gestures in prayer*

The various methods and gestures of prayer have been discussed in detail. The person who prays should strive to make
them his own with the passage of time, so as to practice them
with understanding and at the appropriate times. In that way
he will keep his prayer from becoming "routine, cold, and
shallow".

In particular he should take care to pray in harmony with
the *Church's liturgical year*, and that means not only with
regard to particular hymns, readings, and so on, but also
in what pertains to gestures in prayer. That is to say, he
should make the *serious* character of those days and seasons
that are traditionally designated as days of fast and absti-
nence (Wednesday, Friday, Lent) just as visible (genuflections, metanias) as the *joyful*, festive character of the Lord's
day and of the Easter season.

⌒

These few pages do not claim to exhaust the entire wealth
of what has been handed down from the holy Fathers con-
cerning personal prayer; they do not even come close. They
are intended, as Benedict says of his Rule, only to make a
"beginning".

*But for anyone hastening on to the perfection of [the monastic]
life, there are the teachings of the holy Fathers, the observance of
which will lead him to the very heights of perfection.*

*What page, what passage of the inspired books of the Old and
New Testaments is not the truest of guides for man's life?*

*What book of the holy catholic Fathers does not resoundingly
summon us along the true way to reach our Creator? Then [too,]
the "Conferences" of the Fathers, their "Institutes"[9] and their
"Lives",[10] [and] also the "Rule" of our holy father Basil,[11]*

and all of the other writings of those Fathers who "from the
beginning" walked along that "way" which says of itself,
"I am the WAY"—what are they, if not reliable masters who
will instruct all of those who make the necessary effort to
"set their foot on the same path" and "to accomplish themselves the deeds of the Fathers"?

∽

[9] Two works of John Cassian often cited here.

[10] That is, the Lives of Anthony the Great and other Fathers of monasticism, as well as the *Apophthegmata Patrum*, from which we have drawn
a wealth of quotations.

[11] *Regula Benedicti*, c. 73, 2–5. Translation from *The Rule of St. Benedict
in Latin and English with notes*, ed. Timothy Fry (Collegeville, Minn.,
Liturgical Press, 1981), pp. 295–97.

SOURCES

Besides those already indicated in the footnotes, the following editions and translations were used:

Apophthegmata Patrum: A critical edition of these voluminous and widely ramified materials is not yet available. We have used the Greek text, to the extent that it is accessible (*Gerontikon*; *Evergetinos*; Nau; *Les Apophtegmes des Pères: Collections systématique*, edited by J.-C. Guy, chaps. 1–9, SC 387 [Paris, 1993]). Otherwise we refer the reader to the useful translations of L. Regnault, who brought together the whole material:

> *Les Sentences des Pères du Désert: La Recension de Pélage et Jean*. Solesmes, 1966.
> *Les Sentences des Pères du Désert: Nouveau recueil*. Solesmes, 1970.
> *Les Sentences des Pères du Désert: Troisième recueil*. Solesmes, 1976.
> *Les Sentences des Pères du Désert: Collection alphabétique*. Solesmes, 1981.
> *Les Sentences des Pères du Désert: Série des anonymes*. Bellefontaine, 1985.
> *Les Chemins de Dieu au Désert: La Collection systématique des apophtegmes des Pères*. Solesmes, 1992.

Barsanuphios and John. *Epistulae*. Edited by Nikodemos Hagiorites. (Many editions.) New critical edition (letters 1 to 616 to date): *Barsanuphe et Jean de Gaza: Correspon-*

dence. Edited by F. Neyt and P. de Angelis-Noah. Translated by L. Regnault. SC 426. Paris, 1997; 427: 1998; 450: 2000; 451: 2001. Cf. for the remaining letters: L. Regnault, *Barsanuphe et Jean de Gaza, Correspondence.* Solesmes, 1972.

Clement of Alexandria. *Stromateis.* Edited by O. Stählin. The often quoted book 7 can be found in *Alexandrian Christianity*, edited by J. E. L. Oulton and H. Chadwick. Pp. 93ff. London: SCM Press, 1954.

Evagrius.[1] *De Diversis Malignis Cogitationibus.* Edited and translated by P. Géhin and C. and A. Guillaumont: *Sur les Pensées.* SC 438. Paris, 1998.

———. *De Octo Spiritibus Malitiae.* PG 79, 1145–64. Cf. G. Bunge. *Evagrios Pontikos: Über die acht Gedanken.* Würzburg, 1992. (Translation of the Coislin 109 manuscript.)

———. *De Oratione.* PG 79, 1165–1200. A better text is found in the *Philokalia.* 1:176–89. Athens, 1957. Cf. English translation in *The Philokalia.* Translated by G. E. H. Palmer, Philip Sherrard, and Kallistos Ware. 1:55–71. London, 1979. Cf. also Evagrius Ponticus.

---

[1] Evagrius Ponticus (345–399) was an ascetical writer and an influential figure in fourth-century monasticism. He was ordained a deacon by Gregory of Nazianzen, and John Cassian was one of his disciples for three years. During his lifetime Evagrius was renowned in the East as a spiritual guide. Because of his Neo-Platonic cosmological speculations, some of his works were condemned as being Origenist by several ecumenical councils in the sixth–eighth centuries. Through his disciples and their writings, his teachings on asceticism and prayer contributed to the Church's monastic tradition. Evagrius is quoted twice by the *Catechism of the Catholic Church* (2737, 2742) in the section on prayer. —Trans.

Chapters on Prayer. Translated by J. E. Bamberger. CS 4. Kalamazoo, Mich., 1981.

———. *Epistulae.* Edited by W. Frankenberg. *Evagrius Ponticus.* Berlin, 1912. (Syriac). Translated by G. Bunge: Evagrios Pontikos. *Briefe aus der Wüste.* Trier, 1986.

———. *Praktikos.* Edited by A. and C. Guillaumont: *Traité pratique, ou Le Moine.* SC 171. Paris, 1971. Cf. Evagrius Ponticus. *The Praktikos.* Translated by J. E. Bamberger. CS 4. Kalamazoo, Mich., 1981.

———. *Scholia in Psalmos.* With the gracious permission of M.-J. Rondeau, we use the text that she copied from the manuscript *Vaticanus graecus* 754. Cf. M.-J. Rondeau, *Le Commentaire sur les Psaumes d'Evagre le Pontique.* Pp. 307–48. OCP 26. 1960.

———. *Vita.* Cf. A. de Vogüé and G. Bunge. *Quatre Ermites egyptiens d'après les fragments coptes de l'Histoire Lausiaque.* Pp. 153ff. (*Vie d'Évagre.*) Bellefontaine, 1994.

Hazzaya, Joseph. *Lettre sur les trois étapes de la vie spirituelle.* Edited and translated by P. Harb and F. Graffin. PO 45, no. 202. Turnhout, 1992.

Origen. *De Oratione.* Edited by P. Koetschau. Translated by J. J. O'Meara: *Prayer, Exhortations to Martyrdom.* Ancient Christian Writers 19. New York, 1954.

Pseudo-Justin. *Quaestiones et Responsiones ad Orthodoxos.* PG 6, 1249–1400.

Tertullian. *De Oratione.* Edited by Oehler. Cf. E. Evans. *Tertullian's Tract on Prayer.* London, 1953.

SCRIPTURE INDEX

SUBJECT INDEX